OUTLET GUIDE:
West Coast

OUTLET GUIDE:
West Coast

California, Oregon, and Washington

by A. Miser and A. Pennypincher

A Voyager Book

The Globe Pequot Press

Old Saybrook, Connecticut

Library of Congress Cataloging-in-Publication Data

Miser, A.
   Outlet Guide: West Coast : California, Oregon, and Washington /
by A. Miser and A. Pennypincher. — 1st ed.
     p. cm.
   "A Voyager Book"
   Includes indexes.
   ISBN 1-56440-235-5
   1. Outlet stores—Pacific States—Directories. I. Pennypincher, A.
II. Title
HF5429.215.P13M57 1993
381'.15'02579—dc20   93-19335
                                           CIP

Manufactured in the United States of America
First Edition/Second Printing

Contents

Introduction

In the summer of 1992, in a CBS News Special "Eye On America" report, Dan Rather called factory outlets "the greatest growth segment of retail . . . the wave of the future." In our travels throughout the West Coast of the United States, we found this prediction to be coming true. In the cost-conscious 1990s, factory outlets appear to be the choice of a new generation of bargain shoppers. Individual stores and malls are opening around the United States with amazing frequency. As many of these malls are found outside urban areas, many shoppers travel many miles in search of that illusive bargain. All the outlets we visited were crowded with shoppers and overflowing with discounts unheard of in conventional retail circles. Shoppers reason that if they can pay up to 70 percent less at an outlet for the same item they find at the local department store, why shop at the department store? As more of the general public become aware of the factory outlet phenomenon, the growth of this industry will continue to spiral upward into the next century. Factory outlets offer everything from furniture to fashions, from luggage to lingerie, from china to cosmetics—almost anything you can buy retail can be found in an outlet store somewhere.

History of Outlet Stores

The factory outlet is a natural outgrowth of the manufacturing industry. When faced with the question of what to do with their first-quality overruns, seconds, irregulars, and damaged merchandise, certain manufacturers, mostly in major Midwestern cities and other manufacturing centers, opened stores, usually adjoining their plants, where they offered this excess merchandise for sale to the public. The manufacturers dubbed these new retail entities "factory outlets." As bargain hunters found their way to these stores in increasing numbers, the manufacturers began to make their outlets more attractive to shoppers and to advertise.

The next natural step in the evolution of the factory outlet was the appearance of factory outlet centers—many outlet stores grouped together in the same location. The first outlet center opened in Reading, Pennsylvania, more than fifteen years ago, and since then, shoppers have been coming in droves to these bargain "meccas."

Following the success of outlet centers across the country, real estate developers began the construction of modern factory outlet malls. This phenomenon is finding its full fruition in the 1990s as we see new outlet malls springing up everywhere. Whereas individual outlets still tend to be located in larger cities and older manufacturing centers, outlet malls are usually located along interstates and away from more populated areas in order to avoid competition with department stores that sell goods at retail prices. (California especially has an exceptional number of these malls.) The advantages to shopping at an outlet mall are many, including the great variety of stores (one mall listed in this book has nearly one hundred stores), the abundance of parking, the easy freeway accessibility, and the presence of an assortment of eating establishments within or near the mall. It is now possible to spend an entire day shopping at a local outlet mall!

Planning Your Shopping Trip

In order to enjoy your outlet shopping experience to the fullest, we recommend these simple guidelines:

Before you go shopping, we suggest that you organize a loose-leaf notebook in which you can list all pertinent information about friends and family members for whom you may purchase items. You might want to list individual sizes, favorite styles and colors, preferred brand names, and so forth. You might divide this notebook by setting aside a section for each person for whom you shop. Also, a home section with room-by-room measurements, color schemes, and specific appliance and houseware needs can help you make the most of houseware bargains. Set aside a special section of your notebook for miscellaneous items and new ideas for items you may come across on your factory outlet expedition. Keep the *Outlet Guide: West Coast* with you in the car, in case you find yourself near one of the outlets or outlet malls listed in this book while on vacation. By doing this, you will have the most current information at your fingertips, which will enable you to make intelligent decisions about your shopping destinations.

Timing is also important if you want to have a successful shopping trip. If you are looking for the newest merchandise, it is a good idea to do your shopping early in the week as many outlets receive new shipments of merchandise at this time. By shopping early in the week, you are more likely to find a fine selection of goods. Keep in mind that shopping during weekdays is also a good idea as you avoid the crowds that inevitably flock to factory outlets and outlet malls every weekend. You can avoid the stress and confusion of the crowds and concentrate on getting the most out of your outlet shopping experience by following this simple advice.

Using This Book

1. The Profiles section includes descriptions of what you will find at each outlet. Listed here are the types of merchandise sold and, many times, the percentage discounted off the retail price at that particular outlet. If the outlet is a clothing or shoe outlet, this section will also tell you if it carries men's, women's, or children's fashions or footwear. Use this section to find general information about each store.

2. In the geographic section, cities are listed in alphabetical order under their corresponding states. The states covered in this guide are California, Oregon, and Washington. Individual outlets and malls are then listed under each city. A state map, which is found at the beginning of each section, contains the listings for that state. The cities are numbered on the map so that you can get a clear idea of the location of outlets and malls.

3. Three specialized indexes are found at the end of this book. The Product Index is divided by specific items, such as children's wear, women's fashions, silverware, and so on. By looking up a specific item, you can then find all the outlet stores that carry that particular item. In the Outlet Index, you can look up a particular outlet and find all the cities and towns where that outlet is located. The third index lists the locations of outlet malls.

The authors paid careful attention to the accuracy of the information contained in this book; nevertheless, stores sometimes change their hours and their locations without warning and even go out of business. Be sure to call ahead before planning long-distance travel to any factory outlet. In tourist centers, hours often fluctuate with the tourism season. Most stores accept credit cards and personal checks; when they do not, the listing will so indicate. It is a good idea when paying by check to take along two forms of identification, usually a driver's license and a major credit card. Most individual outlets and malls are accessible to handicapped shoppers; if this is not the case, we have indicated so. Nearby restaurants and the availability of parking for bus tours are also indicated within the individual listings.

Many outlet malls and some individual outlets have mailing lists which inform shoppers of special sales and upcoming events. Some mailings will even include discount coupons. If you are interested in adding your name to one of these mailing lists, simply call the number listed in the mall or individual store listing in this book and inquire. Most will be more than happy to add you to their list.

No outlet owner may purchase a listing in this guide. Inclusion is based on a personal decision by the authors. All information was provided on a purely voluntary basis; consequently, the amount of information varies from profile to profile and from outlet to outlet.

Future editions of this guide will include factory stores that have opened since publication. If you would like to have your store included in the next edition, please write to The Globe Pequot Press, P.O. Box 833, Old Saybrook, CT 06475. References from our readers are welcome.

Factory outlet shopping can be an exciting adventure. One never knows where that next great bargain will be found, but one thing is sure—you are more likely to find it at a factory outlet than at a department store. This guide provides you with the information you will need to find that great bargain as well as all your future great bargains. This guide puts you at an advantage in your bargain-hunting endeavors by telling you how to identify what you want and where to find it. So go out and join "the wave of the future" and save!

Profiles

A&Y Leather Goods
Manufacturers and importers of leatherwear, handbags, briefcases, belts, and wallets, all at discount prices.

Aca Joe
The way casual clothes were meant to feel. An outlet store that features casual and activewear in colorful natural fibers at 25 to 80 percent off for a look that appeals to both men and women.

Accessorize Fashion Jewelry
Savings of 25 to 70 percent from manufacturers to you on fashion jewelry, watches, and accessories.

AC Sport
Factory-direct designer samples and regular stock at wholesale prices.

Activewear Outlet
Save on activewear, sweats, etc., in a variety of styles and colors. Outlet prices every day.

Adler Shoes Outlet
Young contemporary discounted shoes, including Doc Martin, LJ Simone, NY Transit, Zodiac, and more.

Adolfo II
Direct from the manufacturer to you, beautiful ladies' apparel by Adolfo II, Rafael, Donna Toran, and Dressy Tessy at savings to 70 percent.

Adrienne Vittadini
Designer sportswear, accessories, and bed and bath at prices below retail.

AHC Apparel Outlet/Go Silk
Men's and women's separates fresh from the warehouse made from the first-of-its-kind "washable silk." Classic styles from past season. Easy care. Save 50 to 75 percent off regular retail.

Aileen
Ladies' career and casual wear in missy, petite, and plus sizes. Goods are predominately 100 percent cotton and are always first quality. Prices are at least 35 percent below retail.

Albert Nipon
Women's fashions at discount prices.

Alley Kat
Savings of 50 to 80 percent on name-brand fashions, featuring missy (dressy and casual wear), junior sportswear (tops, bottoms, and dresses in all fabrics, including denim), kids, large sizes, and petites.

Altogether
Designer and brand-name sportswear, suits, and dresses.

American Tourister
First-quality luggage and business cases from American Tourister. Sport bags and backpacks from Appalachian Trail. Leather goods from Buxton and much more. Savings up to 70 percent off suggested retail.

Anne Klein
Everyday savings of up to 70 percent off suggested retail on women's fashions, including Anne Klein & Co. and Anne Klein II brands, plus jewelry, watches, and handbags.

Ann Taylor Clearance Center
Career and casual wear for the active and involved woman starting at 50 percent off.

A-1 Furniture Outlet
Furniture and bedding at 10 percent above cost. There is a delivery charge. Will remove old furniture for a small fee.

Apparel Designer Zone
Men's and women's apparel at 40 to 90 percent below retail.

Arrow Factory Store
Arrow dress, sport, and knit shirts, Gold Toe socks, sweaters, pants, ties, and more at great discounts.

ASAP Athletic Shoe Outlet
Athletic shoes for men and women at discount prices.

A Shopping Spree
Save 30 to 70 percent off retail prices on clothing and accessories, including name brands and local children's designer apparel with matching hats in infant, toddler, and 4-to-14 sizes.

Athlete's Foot
Deep discounts on a wide selection of athletic shoes, apparel, and accessories.

Athletic Shoe Outlet
Athletic shoes for men and women, featuring Avia, Bali, Body Glove, Converse, Fila, Kaefa, Keds, L.A. Gear, and Nike at outlet prices.

Audrey Jones
Great savings on women's sportswear and accessories.

Baby Guess?
Factory store for Baby Guess? clothing for children sizes 6 months to 6x at low, low prices.

Bali Importers Outlet
Ladies' wear and accessories imported mainly from Bali and India at a minimum of 70 percent off retail prices.

Ballerini Italian Clothing
Men's clothing directly imported from Italy. High-quality merchandise at 30 to 60 percent less than boutique prices.

Banister Shoes
Big savings every day on famous name-brand shoes. Save on thousands of dress, casual, and athletic styles for both men and women.

Barbie Store
A whole new world of Barbie-for-girls products, each designed with your little girl in mind.

Barbizon Lingerie
In business since 1917. The luxury of fine lingerie at affordable prices featuring Barbizon, Vanity Fair, Eileen West. Daywear/nightwear.

Basic Brown Bear Factory and Store
Basic Brown Bear designs, makes, and sells teddy bears in all shapes and sizes. Because all teddy bears are made on the premises, reasonable savings are passed on to store visitors. Join one of their drop-in tours to see how teddy bears are made and to try the stuffing machine. You can even stuff your own bear starting as low as $8.50!

Basics Beauty Supply & Salon
Professional hair-care products include Paul Mitchell, Redken, Aveda, Nexxus, Lanza, and Focus 21. Nail-care products include Orly, Opi, and Jessica. Also featured are appliances, skin-care products, brushes, combs, hair accessories, and cosmetics. Discount structure: On purchases of $1 to $10, 10 percent off; $10.01 to $20, 20 percent off; $20.01 to $40, 25 percent off; $40.01 or more, 30 percent off. Full service salon and manicurist on premises.

Bass
Factory-direct savings of up to 70 percent on first-quality men's, women's, and children's Bass shoes and accessories, including Weejuns, Bucs, Sunjuns sandals, and other casual styles.

BC Jewelry and Gifts
A collection of local and imported gifts and jewelry. Fashion watches, sterling silver pieces, and leather and evening bags at 20 to 50 percent off retail prices.

Betty's Large Sizes
Moderate designer and brand-name clothing, lingerie, and accessories in sizes 36 to 46 and 14 to 26 at savings up to 50 percent.

Big Dogs Sportswear
Great savings on sportswear for the whole family.

Bijoux Medici
The finest Italian handbags, belts, and accessories at factory-direct prices.

Bizmart
Computers, printers, disk drives, modems, office furniture, and computer accessories all at outlet prices.

Black & Decker
Great savings on power tools, appliances, and accessories.

Bon Worth
Name-brand missy and women's sportswear. Discounts can run up to 90 percent. Bon Worth products are from 30 to 60 percent off regular retail.

Book Warehouse
Books at 50 to 90 percent off publisher's regular retail prices every day. Also computer software and cassettes.

Boot Factory/Genesco
Great savings on boots for both men and women.

Boston Traders
Fine sportswear for men and women at 40 to 50 percent savings off suggested retail.

Brands
Discounted quality apparel and accessories for men and women, all at savings of 30 to 70 percent off retail. Brand names featured are Perry Ellis, Chaps by Ralph Lauren, Nancy Heller, Sanyo, Bill Blass, Michii Moon, Leon Levin, and Lakeland.

Brass Factory Outlet Store
A unique outlet store filled with decorative solid brassware, lamps, nautical items, and more at up to 50 percent off retail.

Bridal Discount Outlet
Wedding gowns, bridesmaids' gowns, prom gowns, *quinceañeras,* and more at discount prices.

Bridal Veil Outlet
Great savings on bridal apparel.

Brindar
Women's fashions at 30 to 70 percent off retail.

Brown Shoe Company Outlet
Women's shoes at savings of 30 to 70 percent.

Bruce Alan Bags
Indulge in luxury leather handbags from the finest designers at savings of 25 to 45 percent off regular retail price. Choose from handbags, accessories, wallets, attaché cases, accessories, and hard-to-find notions.

Bugle Boy
Women's, men's, and kids' wear at 30 to 70 percent off manufacturer's suggested retail price.

Bullock's Clearance Center
Clearance center for the main Bullock's stores. Discounts on men's, women's, and children's clothing and accessories, plus housewares.

Burlington Coat Factory
Great savings on the latest in designer-label fashions, fine linens, and thousands of coats for the entire family.

Byer Factory Outlet
Sportswear and dresses at unbelievable prices.

California Girl Dresses
Factory-direct designer samples and regular stock at wholesale prices.

California Sleepwear Outlet
Ladies' sleepwear and children's clothing, many with smocking and embroidery in regular, large, children's, infant to 6X, and preteen sizes.

Cami'z
Designer/manufacturer and retailer of incomparable cotton sportswear for men, women, and children.

Cape Isle Knitters
The finest in cotton sweaters and knit tops for men and women at outlet prices.

Capezio
Incredible values every day on famous name-brand shoes like Capezio, Liz Claiborne, Pappagallo, Evan-Picone, Esprit, and many more. Current footwear fashions in the latest colors factory direct to you.

Capricorn Coffees
A roasting plant and retail outlet, featuring specialty coffees, teas, and coffee accessories at discount prices.

Carole Hochman Lingerie
Direct from the manufacturer. Everyday savings of 40 to 70 percent on America's leading fashion intimate apparel. Name brands include Christian Dior, Carole Hochman, Sara Beth lingerie, and Lily of France bras.

Carole Little
Famous California designer sportswear for career and sport at 40 percent and more off suggested retail.

Carole's Shoe Heaven
Carole buys stock liquidations, overruns from manufacturers, and clearance inventories. Women's lines include Joan & David, Anne Klein, Via Spiga, MPO, Impo, Caressa, 9 West, Van Eli, and Sesto Meucci. Men's lines include Rockport, Bally, Kenneth Cole, Giorgio Brutini, Bruno Magli, and more.

Carter's Childrenswear
Manufacturer of fine children's wear for more than 125 years. A wide

selection of layette, sleepwear, underwear, and boys' and girls' children's wear at 30 to 60 percent off. Sizes: newborn to girls 6X/boys 7.

Carus
"After-5" and special-occasion dresses and separates. Brand-name suits, dresses, pants, skirts, and blouses at affordable prices.

Casianni
Women's clothing, including leather and suede made in the United States, Nora Ritti Erez, Phillip Noel, and IIF at discount prices.

Catalina
Women's and men's sportswear and swimwear at discount prices.

Centerville USA
Discounts on Western apparel.

Champion Factory Outlet
Substantial savings on activewear for men and women, including first-quality closeout or slightly imperfect sweats, tops, and more in a variety of colors.

Chaus
Save up to 60 percent on Chaus fashion apparel for women including petites and misses sizes.

Chicago Cutlery Etc.
Save on Chicago Cutlery, Magnalite cookware, Wagner cast iron, and more.

Churchill Glove
Manufacturer of full leather work and semidress gloves for men and women. Plus Minnetonka moccasins.

Clothing Clearance Center
Fine menswear up to 70 percent off retail prices.

Coach
Save up to 30 percent for slightly irregular Coach products, including gloves, belts, and handbags.

Cole-Haan
Quality shoes at outlet prices.

Collectibles
A unique collection of designer clothes and accessories for women.

Collectibles Leather
Designer fashions in leather and suede, featuring jackets, skirts, pants, and dresses.

Comfort Connection
Life-style furnishings, including futons, futon frames, tables, lamps, pillows, and accessories at great savings.

Contempo Collection
Specializes in 14K gold, sterling silver, and jade as well as fashion jewelry and gift items priced at $1.00 and above.

Converse
A full line of athletic shoes and clothing for the whole family.

Corning/Corelle
A complete selection of Corelle dinnerware in open stock and sets. Unique coordinating accessories plus discontinued patterns. Hand-crafted glassware, barware, stemware, vases, and giftware at great savings.

Corning/Revere
A wide assortment of Corning Ware, Pyrex, Corelle, Visions, and Revere Ware, open stock and sets. Kitchen gadgets, unique coordinating accessories, seconds, and discontinued patterns at substantial savings.

Cotton Candy
Cotton sportswear featuring a complete line of jeans, pants, shirts, shorts, and activewear. Fashion quality at wholesale prices.

Country Clutter
Great savings on country-style gifts.

Couroc
Monterey's oldest manufacturing company and maker of fine handmade giftware and accessories is famous throughout the world for its unique designs. The factory store carries many award-winning designs, including Monterey Cyprus, Sea Otter, Wharf, Cable Car, Golden Gate Bridge, Poppy, and many more. Savings range from 25 to 75 percent off suggested retail.

Crepe de Chine
Manufacturer's outlet for ladies' silk clothing, including dresses, blouses, skirts, pants, lingerie, and more. Also features large sizes.

Crisa
Save 30 to 70 percent on fine lead crystal and handcrafted glassware, barware, stemware, vases, and much more, featuring Crisa, Clearly, Vitrocrisa, Cufin, Py-o-rey, Boston Warehouse, and M. Kamenstein.

Crystal Works
Elegant accent pieces, home-decorating accessories, and tableware. Significant savings from 20 to 60 percent on Machtmann's finest quality full-lead European crystal.

CYA
Women's fashions at 30 to 70 percent off retail.

Czavra
Designer pure cotton knit coordinates for easy living. Hawaiian cotton and Czavra collection at savings up to 50 percent.

David Textiles Fabric Outlet
Fabrics at savings of 50 to 70 percent off retail, including home decorating, crafts, children's, quilted, velvet, flannel prints, rayon prints, challis prints, calicoes, appliqué prints, linen prints and solids, jacquards, tissue faille prints, cotton prints, polyester prints, poly/cotton prints, sheeting prints and solids, plus many more.

Dehen Knitting Co.
Representing seventy years of tradition in superior-quality knitwear, in-

cluding a line of 100-percent cotton apparel, sweaters, and sport-letter jackets for the entire family at up to 80 percent off retail prices.

Déjà Vu à Paris
Women's fashions and formal wear at discount prices.

The Denim Station
Dressy and casual denim and jeans for men, women, and kids, including name brands such as Levi's, Cross-Colors, Lee, GET Used, Major Damage, and others at savings up to 75 percent off retail.

Designer Brands Accessories
Factory outlet for 1928 jewelry, Laurel Burch, and major handbag, sunglasses, scarf, watch designers/manufacturers. Prices are 30 to 50 percent below department-store prices.

Designer Kids
Unique high-fashion children's wear without the high-fashion price tag. Sizes: boys' newborn up to 8 and girls' newborn all the way to 14.

Designer Labels For Less – Men
A complete collection of name-brand designer suits featuring Jones New York, sport coats, dress slacks and shirts, Italian silk ties, casual wear, and much more, all at 40 to 80 percent off department-store prices.

Designer Labels For Less – Women
Name-brand designer fashions from the Los Angeles Garment Center, featuring Carole Little fashions and Lily of France lingerie.

Designer Man–Woman
A factory outlet featuring California designers. Fashions include name brands like Nina K., Nancy Heller, White on White, Margaret O'Leary Sweaters for women, Z Cavarricci, B.U.M. Equipment, and Guess? Jeans.

Designers' Outlet
Women's clothing, including blouses, dresses, pants, three-piece sets, T-shirts, plus earrings and handbags at up to 50 percent off retail.

Designer's Own
Contemporary, factory-direct sweats, jeans, T-shirts, and shorts.

Desre Exotic Imports
Unique clothing and accessories direct from the island of Bali.

Diamonds Direct
High-quality, 24K-gold jewelry at discount prices.

Direction Menswear
Fashions for today's contemporary man at factory-direct prices.

Discount Fabrics
Savings of 35 to 55 percent off retail on fabrics for home decorating, sportswear, dresswear, threads, and buttons.

Donna Karan Company Store
Women's fashions at 30 to 70 percent off retail.

Dress Barn
Name-brand women's fashions always discounted from 20 to 50 percent. Labels include Liz Claiborne, Silk and Company, Guess?, Nilani, and many more.

Dress Market
International fashions at wholesale prices. Exotic prints in sportswear and dresses in all sizes.

Duffel
Better men's and women's activewear and sportswear featuring Insport workout apparel. Save 50 to 70 percent off retail.

Duffel/Insport
Better casual and active sportswear for men and women in exciting colors and styles. Always discounted at least 50 percent below suggested retail.

Dynasty Imports
Imports from the Orient, including gifts, jewelry, kimonos, women's apparel, and furniture.

Eagle's Eye
Ladies' designer fashions from the famous manufacturer at 40 to 60 percent off. Sportswear, activewear, and career wear in overproduced colors and styles with some irregulars.

East West Concepts
Save 50 to 70 percent off retail prices on women's formal wear, designer wear, sportswear, casual wear, sweaters, knits, and plus sizes.

Eddie Bauer
Save 30 to 70 percent on men's and women's outerwear, sportswear, footwear, and gift items from America's premier outdoor outfitter.

Eddy's for Men
Men's fashions, including shirts, pants, jogging suits, sweaters, jackets, and accessories. Also, silk shirts and ties from Italy and tuxedos and suits, all at great savings.

Eddy's Men's Shoes
Fine designer shoes, including Giorgio Brutini, Pierre Cardin, Freeman, French Shriner, and Aldo Rossini, plus boots and socks—all at outlet prices.

860 Club
Designer labels for less, including Carole Little for Saint Tropez West and Carole Little Petites.

Eileen West Outlet
Eileen West and Queen Anne's lace sleepwear at savings of up to 70 percent off retail. This outlet carries 100-percent cotton and knit signature Eileen West prints and laces with beautiful details and superb quality. One-of-a-kind samples at great prices are also featured.

Elisabeth Stewart
Factory-direct designer samples and slightly imperfect sportswear at prices below wholesale.

Eloise
Better and designer sportswear and dresses in larger sizes.

End of the Line
A clothing manufacturer's outlet store featuring women's activewear, sweaters, casual weekend wear, and jackets, all at 50 to 80 percent off retail.

Ernest of California
Missy and petite designer dresses, suits, and sportswear, including Evan-Picone, Kasper suits, Liz Claiborne dresses, and fashions by Jones New York.

Esprit
Better junior sportswear, kids' wear (including infant, toddler, mini, and teen), footwear, accessories, plus bed and bath. Merchandise is 30 percent off full retail prices—markdowns added regularly as well as "all store" sales at least once a month. No menswear available, but many T-shirt and logo sweatshirt styles are unisex.

Etienne Aigner
Featuring women's first-quality leather footwear, handbags, coats, and accessories at everyday savings from 30 percent off retail prices. Current-season styles and colors as well as selected closeout inventory and sample stock.

Evan-Picone
Savings on an excellent selection of name-brand tailored clothing and sportswear for men and women.

Eve Hair & Beauty Center
Savings on brand-name cosmetics, perfumes, and hair care, featuring Nexxus, Tri Sebastian, KMS, Mastey, Infusium, Tenax, and Focus 21.

Fabric Outlet
All types of dress, upholstery, and drapery fabrics—more than 30,000 square feet of fabrics—"wholesale to the public" at savings of up to 80 percent off the retail price.

Factory
Casual sportswear for men and women at savings of 30 to 50 percent off, including President Stone denim and Parasuco collections.

Famous Brands Housewares
Food preparation items, closet organizational items, food-related textiles, and giftware.

Famous Footwear
Save 10 to 50 percent every day on brand-name athletic dress and casual shoes for the entire family.

Fantastic Sportswear
Paul Stanley regular, petite, and large sizes at wholesale or less. Also, Kenar, Richard & Co., Knit Studio, and Componix.

Fantazi Fashions
Fashion outlet featuring Leslie Fay, Phoebe, and Rabbit Rabbit Rabbit. Also, sportswear, casual wear, leathers, suits, sweaters, and T-shirts.

Farberware
Housewares at 40 percent savings, including Farberware.

Fashion Bin
Teens', missy, casual-to-upgrade clothing at savings of up to 50 percent off retail. Also great savings on watches and jewelry.

Fashion Flair
A collection of well-priced men's, women's, and children's apparel from Izod, Gant, Ship 'n' Shore, and Monet.

Fashion Intuitions
Separates, coordinates, dresses, casual wear, leatherwear; coats and jackets in cottons, rayon, and leather at savings of 50 to 70 percent off retail.

Fashion Show
Dresses, coats, suits, sportswear, including Esprit Sport, all priced below retail.

Fast Clothing
U.S.-made, 100-percent prewashed cotton clothing for casual living at affordable prices.

Fieldcrest Cannon
"Loom to Room" savings of 40 to 60 percent on irregular and discontinued styles. Towels, sheets, blankets, bath rugs, comforters, and more.

Fila
Active sportswear, including tenniswear, golfwear, skiwear, swimwear, workout clothing, denim, and shoes, all at up to 40 percent off retail boutique prices.

Firenze
Contemporary leather and suede sportswear and dresses for women in high-fashion colors by Firenze and Positano. Rugged outerwear for men by M. Julian. Both lines feature new futura leatherwear, which is weatherproof. Also featured is unisex denim sportswear by B. Free. All lines are offered at 30 percent below retail price.

$5 & $10 Store for Women
Great savings on ladies' wear and accessories.

$5 Clothing Store
Great savings on women's clothing. Nothing over $5.

For Men Only
A unique men's sportswear store, featuring the latest fashions at discount prices.

Four Star Apparel Company
Women's apparel at discount prices.

Fragrance World
World-famous men's and women's fragrances, cosmetics, and accessories, all at discounts of 20 to 60 percent off suggested retail prices.

The Framing Center
Custom framing in different styles of molding, including gold leaf, silver leaf, and lacquer finishes; hand-carved and whitewashed exotic and natural woods. The largest selection of Easel Back photo frames in the world. A large selection of ready-made wall frames with glass. All at savings of 30 to 50 percent off retail.

Francine Browner Outlet
Contemporary junior, misses, petite, and large-size sportswear and knits from Francine Browner, Rumours, Workables, Hearts, Monica Heart, D'Knits, Confessions, and Knitables.

Fritzi Outlet
Great savings on girls, kids, junior, missy, petite, and plus-size sportswear and dresses.

Full Size Fashions
Fashion specialists in ladies' sizes 16 and up. Save 25 to 40 percent off name-brand merchandise every day.

Galt Sand
Save 20 to 75 percent on high-quality activewear, sweatshirts, T-shirts, etc.

G & G Nintendo-Sega Outlet
Discounts on Nintendo and Sega software and hardware.

Ganson
Save 20 to 75 percent on women's handbags.

Gant
Updated men's sportswear, featuring dress shirts, sport shirts, knits, rugbys, sweaters, and slacks.

Gap Outlet
The Gap's famous fashionable clothing for men, women, and kids at great prices.

Geoffrey Beene
Specializes in fashions from a popular American designer catering to dress-up, casual, and relaxed life-styles.

Georgiou Outlet
A contemporary collection of career and casual clothing in natural fibers, including raw silk, rayon, wool blends, and cotton at 50 to 80

percent off their retail prices. This is an exclusive outlet for the Georgiou label only.

Gitano
Save on first-quality sportswear and accessories direct from the manufacturer to you. Juniors, misses, plus, maternity, men's, and children's sizes.

The Glassware Outlet
Glass (drinkware, serving, etc.) and candles (basic and with glass holders), all at 25 to 40 percent off.

Gold Corner
Wholesale prices on brand-name, high-fashion costume jewelry and accessories.

Golden Rainbow Outlet
Save on children's clothing, including infant (sizes 0 to 3, 6 to 9, 12, 18, and 24 months), toddler (sizes 2T, 3T, and 4T), boys (sizes 4 to 10) and girls (sizes 4 to 6X). Clothing features European-styled coordinated sportswear for boys and girls at 50 to 75 percent off retail. This 100-percent cotton upscale merchandise is usually found in better department stores. Lines include Golden Rainbow, San Francisco Blues, Spike, and 415.

Gorham
Gorham silver flatware, hollowware, silver pieces, stainless steel and silver-plated flatware; china dinnerware; full lead and fine crystal; also dolls, teddy bears, hand-painted sculptures, musical figurines, Norman Rockwell collectibles, and Christmas ornaments.

Great Goods
The $5 to $20 store—no item more than $20. A large selection of career and casual looks for juniors and women.

Great Outdoor Clothing Co.
Great Outdoor Clothing Co. features the lowest prices on famous-label outdoor clothing—every day, storewide.

Guess?
Guess? jeans for juniors and men at outlet prices.

Gunne Sax Outlet
A large selection of designer dresses, sportswear, evening wear, and children's apparel at savings of 50 to 75 percent off suggested retail prices.

Hanes Activewear
Save on a variety of Hanes activewear styles and colors. Hanes basic sweats for the whole family. First-quality closeouts and slightly imperfects. Everything guaranteed.

Hang Ten
Save 25 percent to 50 percent off manufacturer's suggested retail price on women's and children's clothing.

Happy Times Jewelry
Everyday savings of 20 to 75 percent off retail on 14K gold, gemstones, pearls, diamonds, sterling silver jewelry, fashion jewelry, watches—including Seiko, Pulsar (25 percent off), Anne Klein, Guess? (20 percent off)—and sunglasses—including Ray Ban and Serengetti (25 percent off).

Harry & David
Specialty store includes a wide variety of items from their catalog at discount prices.

harvé benard
Designer clothing for men and women at factory-direct prices.

Hathaway
Famous-maker brand-name dress shirts and sportswear for men at savings up to 30 to 40 percent.

Hawaiian Cotton
Hawaiian Cotton and Czavra Collection includes comfortable designer knits in fashion colors.

Her Lingerie
Imported and domestic fine-quality lingerie at great savings of 30 to 50 percent off retail prices.

He-Ro Group
Women's fashions at 30 to 70 percent off retail.

Home Again
A unique collection of home accessories and quality giftware that reflects traditional decorating trends. Included are table linens, afghans, brass, crystal and silver, framed art, picture frames, stationery, home fragrances, and an ever-changing selection of whimsical gifts for all ages. Truly, a world of affordable treasures, all at outlet prices.

Home Furniture Outlet
Large selection of name-brand sofabeds, sofas, mattresses, and many one-of-a-kind items at savings from 20 to 40 percent off regular retail. Merchandise changes often. Immediate delivery available.

Ian Stewart
Men's designer suits, furnishings, and shoes, including Giorgio Armani, Gianni, Valentino, Courrèges, and Ungaro.

I.B. Diffusion
Contemporary women's apparel at incredible savings.

i.e.
Save on casual footwear for women.

Image Fashion
Up-to-date ladies' dresses, suits, blouses, pants, skirts, blazers, and much more at savings of up to 70 percent off retail prices. Sizes include junior, misses, and large.

In Jewels
Save 50 to 75 percent off regular retail prices on a large selection of earrings, watches, pins, necklace sets, rhinestones, Austrian crystals, and evening handbags.

In 2 Shape
First-quality name-brand women's and children's aerobic, dance, and casual wear at 30 to 70 percent off regular retail prices.

Iona
Save 20 to 75 percent on women's fashions.

Isda & Co.
A wide selection of women's fashions at outlet prices.

IYA
Premier children's wear resource. Clothes that are expressive and fun in girls' sizes 2T to junior 14 and boys' 2T to 7.

Izod
Save up to 50 percent on manufacturer's suggested retail on men's and ladies' Izod sportswear and men's Izod accessories.

Izod/Gant
Save 30 to 50 percent off manufacturer's retail on men's and ladies' Izod/Lacoste fashions and men's Gant dress shirts and sportswear.

Izod/Monet
High-quality fashions direct from the manufacturer for men, women, and children at savings of 30 to 50 percent off manufacturer's suggested retail prices.

Jamis Wear
Quality clothing at affordable prices, including unisex cotton and woolen sweaters and washable silk blouses. Silk blazers and quality jackets are the newest values.

JC Penney Catalog Outlet Store
A totally different kind of JC Penney featuring famous-quality JC Penney merchandise, including overstock and discontinued items from the warehouse and distribution system. Find incredible savings on every-thing from popular fashion to home furnishings. This outlet also maintains a selection of convenience items at everyday, low JC Penney prices.

JC Penney Furniture Warehouse Outlet
A furniture-clearance warehouse for JC Penney with merchandise that includes special-order cancellations, floor models, closeouts, and damaged and returned goods. Prices start at 40 percent off retail and typically are more than 50 percent off.

Jeanne-Marcdowns
Women's fashions at discount prices.

JG Hook
Delightfully affordable prices on this top-quality manufacturer's classic sportswear, including coats and outerwear for misses, petites, and women. Savings run from 30 to 70 percent off retail.

JH Collectibles
An exciting collection of clothing for the fashion-conscious woman. Available in misses and petite sizes.

Jindo Fur
Great values on outerwear options, including beautiful furs, shearlings, leathers, suedes, rainwear, and accessories.

Joan & David Designer Outlet
Savings of up to 70 percent on famous ladies'-designer shoes and accessories.

John Henry & Friends
Fashions for men and women, including Perry Ellis, Thomson, Nino Cerruti, Liberty of London, and John Henry.

Johnston & Murphy
Save 40 to 60 percent on men's shoes, featuring Johnston & Murphy, Sebago, British Walker, Keith Highlander, Bass, and Durango.

Johnston's Fashions for Children
Betti Terral, Fischel, and Petite Gamine children's apparel is discounted from 40 to 60 percent. A true manufacturer's outlet.

Jones New York
The place to shop for incredible savings on women's separates, sportswear, and suits from Jones New York, Jones Sport, and Saville. Everyday savings of up to 75 percent on all merchandise.

Jordache
Designer-label blouses and shirts, denims and slacks, sweaters and jackets, shoes and boots; all first quality and 25 to 70 percent off retail.

Judy's Outlet
Overstock from Judy's stores at huge discounts, including dresses, suits, sportswear, accessories, and Gear for Guys.

Kidswear Center
A wide selection of apparel for boys and girls. Durable quality goods for infants to toddlers, sizes 4 to 6X and 7 to 14, accessories and bows, jewelry, baby gifts, toys, and toy dinosaurs at affordable prices.

Kid's Zone
Save on clothing for children.

Kitchen Collection
Authorized outlet for America's leading brands. Hamilton Beach and Proctor-Silex appliances. Anchor Hocking glassware and Wearever cookware. All at 20 to 70 percent off comparable retail.

Krause's Sofa Factory
Choose from more than 200 styles of made-to-order sofas, recliners, lamps, tables, and fabrics at discount prices. Also save on plants, small entertainment centers, dining sets, china cabinets, and hutches.

Lady N' I
Ladies' and men's leather jackets and coats, ladies' handbags and wallets, men's wallets and gloves, unisex carry-on bags, and more at outlet prices.

L.A. Framing Mart
Custom framing in different styles of molding, including gold leaf, sil-

ver leaf, and lacquer finishes; hand-carved and whitewashed exotic and natural woods. The largest selection of Easel Back photo frames in the world. A large selection of ready-made wall frames with glass. All at savings of 30 to 50 percent off retail.

Larenda Wallets Etc.
Wallets and accessories at discount prices.

L.A. Sox
Designer and fashion socks for men, women, and kids, including Anne Klein, Christian Dior, Tic Tac Toe, and Bonnie Doon.

L.A. Style Activewear
An activewear outlet featuring Baryshnikov, B.U.M., Ray Ban, California Waves, L.A. Movers, and more.

L. Bates Contemporary Clothing
Contemporary designer women's clothing at 35 to 80 percent off regular retail.

L'ccessory
Fashion jewelry and accessories at reasonable prices. Sterling and fashion rings from $3.00. Children's and teens' jewelry, scarves, belts, and hair ornaments.

Leather Express
Men's and women's excellent-quality leather jackets, pants, and skirts for less in glove leather, calfskin, and lambskin.

Leather Loft
Jackets, handbags, luggage, briefcases, wallets, belts, designer accessories, and executive gifts up to 60 percent off retail.

Le Club Handbags
An outlet featuring Sharif, Jay Herbert, Bally, Liz Claiborne, Perry Ellis, Frenchies handbags, plus wallets, hats, gloves, and more.

L'eggs/Hanes/Bali
Famous brand names at savings of up to 50 percent off. Slightly imper-

fects, closeouts, and overstocks of L'eggs and Hanes pantyhose, underwear, socks, Bali lingerie, and more.

Lenore's Fur Outlet
Fine, elegant new designer furs for men and women, including Fendi, Bob Mackie, Adolfo, Bill Blass, and more at savings below wholesale. Most garments are one-of-a-kind and are sold at large markdowns from their regular store prices.

Lenox
Save 40 to 60 percent off retail prices on select seconds of Lenox dinnerware, china, crystal, stemware, handblown items, candles, pewter, and other tabletop accessories and gifts.

Leon Max
Save 20 to 75 percent on women's contemporary sportswear.

Leslie Fay
Savings of 30 to 90 percent off nationally advertised separates, coordinates, better dresses, blazers, sweaters, blouses, shorts and slacks in misses, petites, and women's sizes, featuring Leslie Fay.

Levi's
World-famous jeans and casual clothing for men, women, and children from Levi's.

Lili Ann Outlet
Great savings on women's fashions.

Linen Club
Save on factory-closeout and overstocked bed-and-bath linen and accessories from Wamsutta, Cannon, Fieldcrest, Laura Ashley, Martex, and more.

Linen Factory Outlet
An outlet of Western Linen, Inc., manufacturer, importer, and distributor of textiles for table, kitchen, bed, and bath. These products can be found in some of the finest stores in the country. This outlet features

tablecloths, napkins, placemats, aprons, kitchen towels, potholders, imported British blankets and flannel sheets, comforters, designer pillows, and much more at savings of up to 60 percent below suggested retail.

Lise J
Great savings on women's career and casual wear.

Little Folks Outlet
Children's fashions for boys and girls in sizes newborn to 14.

Liz Claiborne
Substantial savings on wear-now selections. Discontinued first-quality merchandise including dresses and sportswear for misses and petite sizes, handbags and fashion accessories, Claiborne men's sportswear, dress shirts, and neckwear.

London Fog
Substantial savings on a large selection of fine rainwear, jackets, outerwear, and accessories for men and women.

Madelle's
An outlet handling several California Missy manufacturers. Sizes range from 4 to 14 in soft dressing for the workday and weekend wear in tops and bottoms. Also Mickey Mouse apparel. Savings are from 20 to 50 percent off retail.

Magnolia
Sweaters for the contemporary woman featuring designers like Anne Klein and YSI.

Maidenform
Save 30 to 60 percent on first-quality bras, panties, camisoles, slips—all of your lingerie needs. Special savings on holiday weekends.

Malson's Ragsmatazz
Savings of 40 to 60 percent on children's wear, women's wear, shoes, purses, and socks. Also dress pants and jackets.

Marika
Factory-direct savings of 40 to 50 percent on women's and kids' sports-wear by Baryshnikov, Aerodynamics, Marika, and Jazzercise.

Mattel Toy Club
Save 20 to 50 percent on Barbie, Hot Wheels, and Disney preschool and infant toys, all by Mattel.

Maurice Shoes
Name-brand ladies' shoes and handbags at discount prices. Men's shoes, too.

Max Studio
Women's contemporary and updated sportswear direct from the manu-facturer.

McKenzie Outfitters
Quality outdoor clothing and equipment from major manufacturers. Save 20 to 50 percent on sweats, sweaters, socks, jackets, Gore-Tex rain-wear, and athletic or hiking footwear.

Men at Work
Designer suits, slacks, sport coats, Italian shoes, silk and cotton shirts, sweaters, and accessories at great savings.

Mikasa
Save up to 60 percent on fine crystal, china, giftware, stemware, cook-ware, flatware, and much, much more.

Mill Valley Cotton Outlet
High-quality 100-percent cotton sportswear for women in sizes small, medium, large, and one-size-fits-all at savings of 50 to 70 percent off re-tail price. All items are preshrunk and garment-dyed. This outlet offers a wide selection of jumpsuits, dresses, jackets, pants, shorts, skirts, and more in beautiful colors. They are designed to be versatile and can be paired together in many combinations.

Mom's Gallery Children's Boutique
European designer clothes for infants, girls' sizes 0 to 14 and boys' 0 to 16, plus maternity fashions—most below wholesale.

Mousefeathers Factory Store
One-hundred-percent cotton dresses and jumpsuits in sizes 12M to 14 in original prints designed by Mousefeathers. A large selection of coordinating accessories—including headbands, hats, shoes, and socks—are also featured. Merchandise varies seasonally. All at savings of up to 75 percent off retail price.

Multiple Choices
Brand-name women's, men's, boys', girls', and infants' clothing at outlet prices.

Multiples
Famous fashion knits designed for the woman on the go. One size fits all.

Mushrooms
Mushrooms, Red Cross, and more in women's dress and casual shoes. Brand names at 33 percent and more off regular retail.

My Place
Fine men's socks, tote bags, travel bags, and Samsonite luggage at discount prices.

Nathan J. Children's Wear
One-hundred-percent Pima cotton clothing and accessories for infants and children to size 7 at factory-direct prices.

Natural Footgear
Name-brand contemporary comfort casual and outdoor footwear for men and women up to 40 percent off retail. Everyday values on brands like Timberland, Dexter, Sperry, and Eastland.

Naturalizer
Save on shoes for women.

Newport Outlet
Direct imports from silk factories in the Orient. Machine and hand washable. Silk jackets, tops, scarves, and many other beautiful silk garments.

New West
Contemporary men's and women's sportswear, shoes, belts, and hats at up to 60 percent off retail.

New York Cosmetics & Fragrances
Deeply discounted cosmetics and fragrances. Save 10 to 70 percent off retail.

New York Express
Save on jewelry and accessories.

Next Express
Home and office furniture, including contemporary designs at 20 to 70 percent off. Also, floor samples, closeouts, and Budget End Furnishings.

Nike
Discontinued and irregular athletic shoes, apparel, and accessories, all at factory-store prices.

9 West
Footwear at savings of 30 percent and more every day. Hundreds of styles to choose from.

Nordstrom Rack
This off-price division of Nordstrom features savings of 30 to 50 percent off retail on men's, women's, and children's shoes, men's clothing and sportswear, children's casual, ladies dresses, sportswear, juniors, accessories, and lingerie. This store also serves as a clearance center for the main Nordstrom stores.

Norm Thompson
Women's fashions at 30 to 70 percent off retail.

North Face Factory Outlet
Great savings of 20 to 70 percent on skiwear, down and fleece clothing, windwear, rainwear, backpacks, tents, sleeping bags, long underwear, socks, sportswear, and more.

Old Mill
First-quality ladies' fashions at 25 to 70 percent off the manufacturer's suggested retail prices. Sizes 4 to 18; petites 4 to 16.

Olga/Warner
Famous-maker brand-name women's intimate apparel, daywear, sleepwear, and more at 30 to 50 percent off retail prices.

Omid International Rugs
Manufacturer and importer of Oriental rugs from Persia and China. Runner to room size—unmatched at any price.

Oneida
Huge savings from one of the world's leading makers of fine tableware. Includes stainless flatware, silver-plated flatware, baby items, and other fine gifts.

OshKosh B'Gosh
OshKosh B'Gosh sportswear for the entire family at considerable savings.

Outback
Save on casual women's apparel. "Beauty and comfort with a flattering fit."

Outerwear Company
A unique outlet for men and women with the finest updated designer leatherwear and Icelandic wool sweaters and jackets. A beautiful selection of novelty jackets, all-weather jackets, and leather handbags.

Outlet for Contemporary Career Clothing
Women's apparel at outlet prices.

Paper Factory/Paper Outlet
Your value party-and-paper store. Everyday low prices on party goods,

decorations, balloons, giftwrap, bags, bows, ribbon, greeting cards, invitations, books, games, puzzles, and home, office, and school supplies.

Party America
Great savings on greeting cards, party goods, and office supplies.

Patagonia
Women's fashions at 30 to 70 percent off retail.

Paul Jardin
Direct from the manufacturer—first-quality men's apparel and accessories including ties, shirts, sweaters, shoes, and more.

Paul Stanley Ltd.
Factory store featuring jackets, skirts, pants, silk blouses, dresses, and coats in regular, petite, and large sizes. Prices always below wholesale.

Perfumania
Save 20 to 60 percent on a variety of the world's top brand-name men's and women's fragrances and cosmetics.

Perry Ellis
Perry Ellis shoes and accessories at prices 25 to 70 percent off suggested retail.

Pfaltzgraff
Offering direct from the factory a large selection of casual dinnerware as well as a vast array of complementary tabletop accessories.

PFC Fragrance & Cosmetics
World-famous brands of men's and women's fragrances, toiletries, cosmetics, and accessories at 25 to 70 percent off retail prices.

Philippe Simon
A large selection of American designers, including Nina K., Cline Kolarek, Yes, Cafe, Jonathan Martin, and Arrested at up to 70 percent off retail.

Politix

Private-label European menswear, including jackets, trousers, shirts, shoes, accessories, and casual wear (including denim) at 30 to 70 percent below original prices.

Polly Flinders

Save 30 to 60 percent on world-famous Polly Flinders dresses. Sizes newborn to 14. Selected sportswear for boys and girls also available.

Polo/Ralph Lauren

Men's, women's, children's, and home collections.

Prestige Fragrance & Cosmetics

Famous-maker designer-label fragrances, cosmetics, and personal-care products for men and women at 20 to 60 percent off retail. Cosmetic accessories include cosmetic bags, atomizers, and bath products.

Prime Time

Wholesalers and importers of Swiss and Japanese brand-name watches and French and Italian brand-name sunglasses. Manufacturer of fine jewelry at factory-direct prices.

Publishers Outlet

An outlet featuring publishers' high-quality limited-availability remnant books. Selected gift books, children's books, cookbooks, videos, and more are priced at 30 to 75 percent below retail every day.

Rainbeau Bodywear

Exercise wear, including leotards, exercise pants, etc., at savings of 20 to 75 percent off retail prices.

Rawlings Sporting Goods

"The Mark of the Pro." NFL-licensed apparel and equipment plus Rawlings sports equipment and clothing at 40 to 60 percent off suggested retail prices.

Reebok

Save 20 to 50 percent off suggested retail prices on all Reebok and Avia athletic footwear, apparel, and accessories for men, women, and children.

The Ribbon Outlet, Inc.
Factory-direct savings on more than 3,000 varieties of first-quality ribbons and trims. Cut your own "by-the-yard," precut, or entire spools in bulk. Selected craft supplies, bridal and hair accessories. Wearable Arts items also available.

Ritch Street Outlet
Designer kitchen and dining linens, including placemats, napkins, tablecloths, aprons, canvas bags, bread keepers; ceramic cookware, porcelain dishes, music boxes, coasters, and handmade dolls from well-known manufacturers selling to better stores. Most items are priced at wholesale.

Robert Scott/David Brooks
Women's fashions at 30 to 70 percent off retail.

Rock Express
Rock T-shirts, sweatshirts, memorabilia, designer garments, and accessories at up to 80 percent off retail.

Royal Doulton
Save 20 to 70 percent on a prestigious assortment of china, giftware, figurines, and crystal. Includes best quality and value-oriented seconds. Special orders accepted.

Royal House
Discount sterling silver jewelry, including Benrus watches, sunglasses, souvenir gifts, T-shirts, and cards.

Royal Robbins
Outdoor and casual clothing for men and women at 20 to 70 percent off retail. The Royal Robbins line includes sweaters, belts, hats, skirts, pants, shorts, dresses, shirts, and tops, most made from 100 percent cotton or other natural fibers in many distinctive patterns and weaves. Many styles are unisex.

Ruff Hewn
Save 35 to 50 percent off retail on rugged, comfortable sportswear for men and women who lead an active life-style.

Rug Resource
Savings of 50 to 80 percent on Oriental rugs of every size and description.

Salina Fashion
Brand-name women's apparel and accessories at 50 to 75 percent off retail prices.

Salon de Beauté
Full-service hair salon, featuring Nexxus, Sebastian, Paul Mitchell, as well as cosmetics and fragrances for men and women at discount prices.

Sam & Libby
Great savings on women's footwear.

Sandra Ingrish Outlet
Women's apparel, including samples, short sets, skirts, pants, camp shirts, blouses, cardigans, shorts, tops, and miscellaneous at savings of up to 40 percent off retail. Sizes include petite, misses, and large.

San Francisco City Lights Outlet
A huge selection of cotton/Lycra (90/10) bodywear, dancewear, and streetwear; 100-percent-cotton sportswear, activewear, and kids' wear; irregulars and closeouts, all at 35 to 60 percent off retail.

Saratoga Sport Outlet
Contemporary women's sportswear as seen in department stores at unbeatable prices—50 to 80 percent off retail.

Sassafras
Housewares, gifts, and contemporary life-style products for adults and children at savings of 10 to 50 percent.

Sbicca Shoes
Women's casual footwear—the latest styles at factory-direct prices.

Scott's Fifth Avenue
Quality contemporary and traditional fashion jewelry carried by all major department stores at outlet prices. Also, pearls and Swarovski crystal.

Sears Outlet
Values for the entire family, including clothing, shoes, housewares, home furnishings, and appliances at 20 to 70 percent off catalog prices.

Sergio Tacchini
Great savings on fashions for men and women.

SF Fashion Outlet
Women's clothing includes brands not found in other outlets. Current merchandise is 50 percent off retail price.

Shoe Outlet
Shoes for men, women, and children at outlet prices.

Shoe Pavilion
Great savings on men's and women's footwear.

Sierra Shirts
Casual printed sportswear in sizes, colors, and styles to fit the entire family. Manufacturer direct. Reduced prices on all items.

Silver & More
Save on silver giftware and accessories.

Simply Cotton
Save on comfortable women's casual wear.

Sister Sister
Fun contemporary clothing for size 14 and beyond at factory outlet prices.

Six Star Factory Outlet
A general variety outlet where no item retails for more than $10. Save 25 to 75 percent off regular retail prices every day on cosmetics, greet-

ing cards, toiletries, party goods, stationery, housewares, toys, shirts, pictures, frames, novelties, gifts, and more.

Socks Galore
A sock-lover's dream. More than 60,000 pairs at 25 to 80 percent off retail.

SpaGear
Women's sportswear, bathing suits, jogging suits, etc., at 30 to 70 percent off retail prices.

Spare Changes
Better women's and children's wear at 40 to 80 percent below retail prices. This outlet carries designer-label career clothing, dresses, jumpsuits, and sportswear in petite (2 to 14), women's (4 to 18) and junior (3 to 13) sizes. Also featured are infants', children's, and toddlers' clothing.

Sparkle Plenty Too
Handcrafted fashion jewelry manufactured on-site and sold to department stores around the country. Savings of 50 percent or more on earrings, sunglasses, belts, purses, and beads and parts to make your own jewelry.

Sportif USA
Athletic wear for men and women at outlet prices.

Sports Mania Outlet
Sports jackets, caps, and T-shirts with licensed official insignias.

Star Baby
Everyday savings of up to 50 percent on clothing plus accessories for newborns and children to size 7.

Stubbies Outlet
Great savings on men's apparel.

Studio Two
Original designs in glass at outlet prices.

Sunglass World
Save up to 25 percent on national-brand sunglasses including Ray Ban, Serengetti, Eyescreens, Porsche, and more.

Swank
Accessories and designer costume jewelry for men and women at deep factory discounts.

The Sweatshirt Company
A colorful selection of sweats and knit sportswear, including adult, youth, and big and tall sizes at outlet prices.

Tabari Collection
Designer fashions, special-occasion dresses, silk dresses, suits, sports-wear, shoes, and furs at a discount.

Talbot's
Save on ladies' clothing including sportswear, career wear, and accessories.

Tanner Factory Store
A significant selection of classic ladies' apparel for less than you would expect.

THE Housewares Store
Flatware and dinnerware accessories, cutlery and kitchen gadgets, glassware and acrylics, bakeware and cookware, grills, baby gifts, lamps, and more.

Ticket Sportswear
Young designer sportswear at 50 to 70 percent off retail.

Tight End
Fitness and body wear for men and women at outlet prices.

T.J.'s Factory Store
Bridal and designer clothing for the fashionable woman at discount prices.

Today's Child
Sportswear, sleepwear, dresses, accessories, and layette at outlet prices in boys' sizes infant to 7 and girls' infant to 14.

totes Factory Stores
Save up to 70 percent every day on famous totes' umbrellas, raincoats, rain hats, luggage, bags, and more.

Townsend Clearance Center
Women's clothing in junior, missy, and large sizes. Nothing more than $30.

Toy Liquidators
Save 40 to 70 percent on name-brand toys, including Mattel, Playskool, Nintendo, and Hasbro.

Toys Unlimited
Great savings on a wide variety of toys for children of all ages.

Trend Club
A discount specialty retailer that sells apparel to junior-size women at 20 to 50 percent below department-store prices.

Troy Shirt Makers Outlet
Manufacturer's outlet of premium-quality men's dress shirts, sport shirts, formal wear, robes, and pajamas at 40 to 70 percent off retail prices.

Ultimate Boutique
Impressive selection of quality women's clothing to satisfy women with diverse fashion tastes. Women's suits, dresses, evening wear, separates, accessories, and handbags at 50 percent off retail price. Sizes 4 to 18.

Unique Jewelry
High-fashion jewelry plus hats, scarves, hair accessories, watches, and batteries. Also styles for brides and bridesmaids.

United Colors of Benetton
Clothing in internationally famous styles and colors at 30 to 75 percent off regular store prices for men, women, and children.

UP Fashion Clearance Center

Fashions for women and juniors at savings of 50 to 75 percent off retail prices. Gifts at savings of 25 to 75 percent off retail. Women's accessories at savings of 50 to 80 percent off retail.

Upholstery Fabric Outlet (UFO)

Decorative fabrics for the home, including upholstery and drapery fabrics, supplies, and zippers. A huge selection at up to 50 percent off retail.

Van Heusen

An extensive selection of dress shirts, accessories, and sportswear for men and women at manufacturer-direct savings of 20 to 50 percent.

Vanity Fair

Lee, Vanity Fair, Barbizon, Health-Tex, JanSport, Jantzen, Vassarette, and more. Jeans, lingerie, sportswear, daywear, loungewear, swimwear, and workwear for the entire family.

Wallet Works

Wallets and billfolds handcrafted in America at great values. Plus luggage, handbags, belts, portfolios, attaché cases, and travel gifts.

Welcome Home

A unique collection of home accessories and quality giftware reflecting traditional decorating styles. Included are table linens, afghans, brass, crystal and silver, framed art, picture frames, stationery, home fragrances, and an ever-changing selection of whimsical gifts for all ages. Truly, a world of affordable treasures, all at outlet prices.

Wemco

The world's largest tie manufacturer offers more than 10,000 neckties in all colors and styles along with the most updated men's sportswear. Save 40 to 80 percent every day.

West Point Pepperell

Linens, apparel, and home-decorating accessories with brand names like Atelier, JP Stevens, Martex, Lady Pepperell, Utica, and Esprit. Savings range from 20 to 70 percent.

Westport Ltd.
Top-quality labels for the career woman in suits, dresses, sportswear, and separates. Always 20 to 50 percent below department-store prices.

Westport Woman
Women's fashions sizes 14W to 24W, always at 20 to 50 percent off department-store prices.

Whims-Sarah Coventry Outlet
Lifetime-guaranteed jewelry, Sarah Coventry fashion accessories, watches, wallets, and hair goods.

Wicker Factory
Tremendous savings on high-quality wicker, silk plants, custom arrangements, and home decor.

Windsor Fashions
Fine designer and contemporary wear for men and women. A large collection of current styles in suits, sportswear, and dresses.

Wisconsin Toy
Save 20 to 75 percent on name-brand toys.

Women's Fashions
Dresses for every occasion, including beaded evening dresses, blouses, sweaters, and jackets.

California

Numbers to the left of entries in this legend correspond to the numbers on the accompanying maps. The number to the right of each city's or town's name is the page number on which that municipality's outlets first appear.

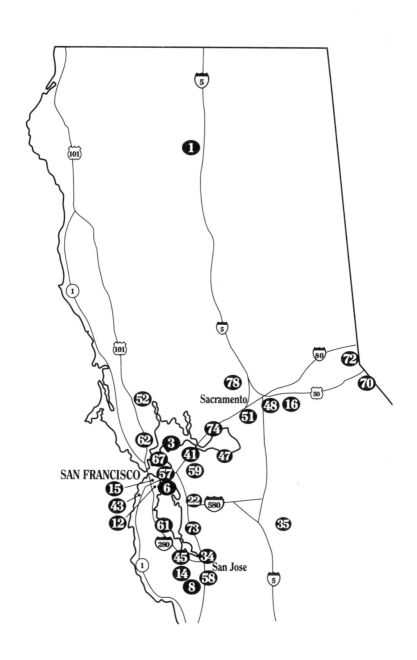

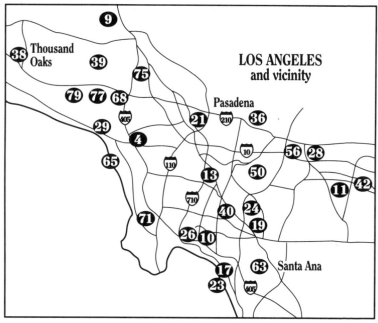

Anderson

Shasta Factory Outlets
State Highway 273 and Deschutes Road

Directions: Take I–5 and exit at Deschutes (State Route 273).
Phone: (916) 378–1000
Hours: Summer: 9:30 A.M.–8:00 P.M., Monday–Saturday; 11:00 A.M.–6:00 P.M., Sunday. Winter: 9:30 A.M.–6:00 P.M., Monday–Saturday; 11:00 A.M.–6:00 P.M., Sunday.
Outlets:
Aileen
Banister Shoes
Bass
Book Warehouse
Bugle Boy
Cape Isle Knitters
Corning/Revere
Designer Brands Accessories
Duffel
Famous Footwear
Fieldcrest Cannon
Full Size Fashions
Gitano
harvé benard
Home Again
Izod/Gant
Kitchen Collection
Leather Loft
L'eggs/Hanes/Bali
Levi's
London Fog
Mikasa
Oneida
Perfumania
Polly Flinders
The Ribbon Outlet, Inc.
Sunglass World

The Sweatshirt Company
totes Factory Stores
Toy Liquidators
Van Heusen
Vanity Fair
Wallet Works
Westport Ltd.
Whims-Sarah Coventry Outlet
Credit Cards: Most major cards accepted.
Personal Checks: Most stores accept checks with proper identification.
Handicapped Accessible: Yes
Food: Snack Time restaurant in mall
Bus Tours: Yes
Notes or Attractions: Eight miles south of Redding

Barstow

Factory Merchants Outlet Mall
2837 Lenwood Road

Directions: Located halfway between Los Angeles and Las Vegas. Take the Lenwood Road exit off the 15 Freeway just south of Barstow.
Phone: (619) 253–7342
Hours: 9:00 A.M.–8:00 P.M., Monday–Sunday
Outlets:
Aca Joe
Adolfo II
Aileen
Anne Klein
Banister Shoes
Barbizon Lingerie
Bass
Big Dogs Sportswear
Black & Decker
Book Warehouse
Boot Factory/Genesco
Bruce Alan Bags

Bugle Boy
Capezio
Chicago Cutlery Etc.
Coach
Corning/Revere
Designer Brands Accessories
Eagle's Eye
Evan-Picone
Fieldcrest Cannon
Gant
Gitano
Hanes Activewear
Izod/Monet
John Henry & Friends
Johnston & Murphy
Jones New York
Kitchen Collection
Leather Loft
L'eggs/Hanes/Bali
Lenox
Levi's
London Fog
Oneida
OshKosh B'Gosh
Paper Factory/Paper Outlet
Perfumania
Polly Flinders
Polo/Ralph Lauren
Rawlings Sporting Goods
Reebok
The Ribbon Outlet, Inc.
Royal Doulton
Ruff Hewn
Sergio Tacchini
Socks Galore
Swank
Toys Unlimited
Van Heusen

Wallet Works
Welcome Home
Credit Cards: Most major cards
Personal Checks: Most stores accept checks with proper identification.
Handicapped Accessible: Yes
Food: Lunch Break eatery in mall
Bus Tours: Yes

Berkeley

Home Furniture Outlet
1099 Ashby Avenue

Directions: Take I–80 to the Ashby Avenue exit. Go 2 long blocks; the outlet is on the left side of the street at the corner of San Pablo Avenue. It is a part of a big complex.
Phone: (510) 486–8000
Hours: 10:00 A.M.–6:30 P.M., Monday–Thursday; 10:00 A.M.–6:00 P.M., Friday–Saturday; 11:30 A.M.–5:30 P.M., Sunday
Credit Cards: Discover, MasterCard, Visa
Personal Checks: Yes
Handicapped Accessible: Yes
Food: One mile away
Bus Tours: Yes
Notes or Attractions: Near University Art Museum, University of California, Berkeley campus, and Berkeley Rose Garden

Mousefeathers Factory Store
1001 Camellia Street

Directions: Exit Gilman Street off I–80 East; located at the corner of Ninth and Camellia.
Phone: (510) 526–0261
Hours: 9:30 A.M.–5:00 P.M., Tuesday–Saturday
Credit Cards: MasterCard, Visa
Personal Checks: Yes
Handicapped Accessible: Yes

Food: Within 2 blocks
Bus Tours: Yes
Notes or Attractions: Near several clothing, gardening, and other retail outlets

New West
2967 College Avenue

Directions: Take the I–80 to 80 North and exit Ashby; located at the corner of Ashby and College.
Phone: (510) 849–0701
Hours: 11:00 A.M.–6:00 P.M., Monday–Saturday; 11:00 A.M.–5:00 P.M., Sunday
Additional Savings: Seasonal markdowns
Credit Cards: American Express, MasterCard, Visa
Personal Checks: Yes
Handicapped Accessible: Yes
Food: On the same block
Bus Tours: No
Notes or Attractions: The University of California, Berkeley, is nearby.

North Face Factory Outlet
1238 Fifth Street

Directions: Take I–80 and exit Gilman Street. Go 5 blocks east.
Phone: (510) 526–3530
Hours: 10:00 A.M.–6:00 P.M., Monday–Wednesday, Friday–Saturday; 10:00 A.M.–8:00 P.M., Thursday; 11:00 A.M.–5:00 P.M., Sunday
Additional Savings: Monthly specials as well as three large sales events a year
Credit Cards: American Express, Discover, MasterCard, Visa
Personal Checks: Yes
Handicapped Accessible: Yes
Food: One to 3 blocks away
Bus Tours: No

Outback
2517 Sacramento Street

Directions: Take Ashby Avenue off I–80; turn left onto Sacramento. Located just before Dwight Way on Sacramento.
Phone: (510) 548–4183
Hours: 11:00 A.M.–7:00 P.M., Monday–Friday; 10:00 A.M.–6:00 P.M., Saturday; 11:00 A.M.–5:00 P.M., Sunday
Credit Cards: MasterCard, Visa
Personal Checks: Yes
Handicapped Accessible: Yes
Food: Nearby
Bus Tours: Yes
Notes or Attractions: Near University of California, Berkeley

Royal Robbins
841-A Gilman Street

Directions: From San Francisco, follow I–80 East across the Bay Bridge to the Gilman Street exit and head east.
Phone: (510) 527–1961
Hours: 10:00 A.M.–6:00 P.M., Monday–Wednesday, Friday–Saturday; 10:00 A.M.–8:00 P.M., Thursday; 11:00 A.M.–5:00 P.M., Sunday
Additional Savings: Occasional major "$5 Blowout" sales, often at the whim of the store manager
Credit Cards: MasterCard, Visa
Personal Checks: Yes
Handicapped Accessible: Yes
Food: Nearby
Bus Tours: No
Notes or Attractions: Major shopping mecca for bargain hunters; many factory outlets nearby

Beverly Hills

Lenore's Fur Outlet
223 South Beverly Drive #200

Directions: Located in the second block south of Wilshire on the west side of the street. Main cross streets are Wilshire and Olympic.
Phone: (310) 278–4001
Hours: 10:00 A.M.–5:00 P.M., Monday–Saturday or by appointment
Credit Cards: American Express, MasterCard, Visa
Personal Checks: Yes
Handicapped Accessible: No
Food: Many very good restaurants are located on this street.
Bus Tours: Yes
Notes or Attractions: Rodeo Drive is 1 block west, featuring many wonderful shops and beautiful buildings. The Beverly Wilshire Hotel is 2 blocks away.

Bishop

Home Again
1180 North Main Street #6

Directions: Call ahead.
Phone: (619) 872–3422
Hours: Call ahead for hours.
Credit Cards: American Express, Discover, MasterCard, Visa
Personal Checks: Yes
Handicapped Accessible: Yes
Food: Nearby
Bus Tours: Yes

Brisbane

Aca Joe
235 Valley Drive

Directions: Call ahead.
Phone: (415) 467–4450
Hours: 10:00 A.M.–5:00 P.M., Monday–Saturday; noon–5:00 P.M., Sunday
Credit Cards: American Express, Discover, MasterCard, Visa
Personal Checks: Yes
Handicapped Accessible: Yes
Food: Within minutes
Bus Tours: Yes

Fila
145 Park Lane

Directions: Call ahead.
Phone: (415) 468–6800
Hours: 10:00 A.M.–5:00 P.M., Monday–Saturday; noon–5:00 P.M., Sunday
Credit Cards: American Express, MasterCard, Visa
Personal Checks: Yes
Food: Nearby
Bus Tours: Yes

Cabazon

Desert Hills Factory Stores
48650 Seminole Road

Directions: From eastbound I–10, exit Fields Road; turn left, then right.
From westbound I–10, exit Apache Trail; turn right, then left.
Phone: (714) 849–6641
Hours: 9:00 A.M.–8:00 P.M., Monday–Sunday
Outlets:
Adolfo II
Adrienne Vittadini

Aileen
Albert Nipon/Leslie Fay
American Tourister
Anne Klein
Barbizon Lingerie
Bass Shoes
Capezio
Corning/Revere
Czavra
Designer Brands Accessories
Donna Karan Company Store
Duffel
Eddie Bauer
Esprit
Evan-Picone
Famous Footwear
Full Size Fashions
Gant
Geoffrey Beene
Gitano
Gorham
Guess?
Hanes Activewear
harvé benard
He-Ro Group
Joan & David Designer Outlet
John Henry & Friends
Johnston's Fashions for Children
Jones New York
Kitchen Collection
Leather Loft
L'eggs/Hanes/Bali
Maidenform
Nike
Oneida
Paper Factory/Paper Outlet
Patagonia
Perry Ellis

Pfaltzgraff
The Ribbon Outlet, Inc.
Robert Scott/David Brooks
Royal Doulton
Socks Galore
SpaGear
Tanner Factory Store
Toy Liquidators
Van Heusen
Wallet Works
Welcome Home
West Point Pepperell
Credit Cards: Most major cards
Personal Checks: Most stores accept checks with proper identification.
Handicapped Accessible: Yes
Food: A variety of restaurants are located in the mall, including The Bakery at Desert Hills, China Hut, Coffee All You Want/Scrubbed Potato, Moondoggies, Salsa The Border, and Valentino's Italian Eatery.
Bus Tours: Yes; special programs for tour groups

Campbell

Six Star Factory Outlet
Campbell Plaza
2425 Winchester Boulevard

Directions: Call ahead.
Phone: (408) 379–7769
Hours: 9:30 A.M.–8:00 P.M., Monday–Friday; 9:30 A.M.–7:00 P.M., Saturday; 11:00 A.M.–6:00 P.M., Sunday
Credit Cards: MasterCard, Visa
Personal Checks: Yes
Handicapped Accessible: Yes
Food: Available in the vicinity
Bus Tours: Yes

Canyon Country

Krause's Sofa Factory
18821 Soledad Canyon Road

Directions: Call ahead.
Phone: (805) 251–1315
Hours: 10:00 A.M.–9:00 P.M., Monday–Friday; 10:00 A.M.–6:00 P.M., Saturday–Sunday
Additional Savings: Semiannual sale (two per year)
Credit Cards: Discover, MasterCard, Visa
Personal Checks: Yes
Handicapped Accessible: Yes
Food: In the vicinity
Bus Tours: No

Cerritos

Krause's Sofa Factory
17512 Studebaker Road

Directions: Call ahead.
Phone: (310) 924–7871
Hours: 10:00 A.M.–9:00 P.M., Monday–Friday; 10:00 A.M.–6:00 P.M., Saturday and Sunday
Additional Savings: Semiannual sale (two per year)
Credit Cards: Discover, MasterCard, Visa
Personal Checks: Yes
Handicapped Accessible: Yes
Food: In the vicinity
Bus Tours: No

Chino

Nordstrom Rack
5537 Philadelphia Street

Directions: Call ahead.
Phone: (714) 591–0551
Hours: 10:00 A.M.–9:00 P.M., Monday–Friday; 10:00 A.M.–8:00 P.M., Saturday; 11:00 A.M.–6:00 P.M., Sunday
Additional Savings: Legendary 25-percent and 50-percent off sales
Credit Cards: American Express, MasterCard, Nordstrom, Visa
Personal Checks: Yes, with two pieces of identification
Handicapped Accessible: Yes
Food: Nearby
Bus Tours: Yes; call ahead for information.

Colma

Fila
280 Metro Center
63 Colma Boulevard

Directions: Call ahead.
Phone: (415) 992–3777
Hours: 10:00 A.M.–8:00 P.M., Monday–Friday; 10:00 A.M.–6:00 P.M., Saturday; noon–6:00 P.M., Sunday
Credit Cards: American Express, MasterCard, Visa
Personal Checks: Yes
Handicapped Accessible: Yes
Food: Nearby
Bus Tours: Yes

Commerce

Catalina Outlet
6015 Bandini Boulevard

Directions: Call ahead.
Phone: (213) 724–4693
Hours: 9:00 A.M.–5:00 P.M., Monday–Friday; 9:00 A.M.–4:00 P.M., Saturday; 11:00 A.M.–5:00 P.M., Sunday
Credit Cards: MasterCard, Visa
Personal Checks: Yes (California only)
Handicapped Accessible: Yes
Food: In the vicinity
Bus Tours: Yes

Citadel Outlet Collection
5674 East Telegraph Road

Directions: From Los Angeles, exit I–5 at Washington; go left and left again on Telegraph Road. From San Diego and Orange County, exit I–5 at Atlantic Boulevard North.
Phone: (213) 888–1220
Hours: 10:00 A.M.–8:00 P.M., Monday–Saturday; 10:00 A.M.–6:00 P.M., Sunday
Outlets:
Adolfo II
Aileen
Ann Taylor Clearance Center
Bijoux Medici
Book Warehouse
Capezio
Corning/Corelle
Corning/Revere
Designer Labels For Less – Men
Designer Labels For Less – Women
Designer's Own
Desre Exotic Imports
Direction Menswear

Eddie Bauer
Firenze
Francine Browner Outlet
Full Size Fashions
Gap Outlet
Gitano
harvé benard
Hawaiian Cotton/Czavra Collections
In 2 Shape
Joan & David Designer Outlet
Kitchen Collection
Leather Loft
L. Bates Contemporary Clothing
Linen Club
Max Studio
Multiples
Nathan J. Children's Wear
Paul Jardin
Perry Ellis
Politix
Prestige Fragrance & Cosmetics
Prime Time
Sbicca Shoes
Socks Galore
Star Baby
Toy Liquidators
Troy Shirt Makers Outlet
United Colors of Benetton
Welcome Home
Whims-Sarah Coventry Outlet
Credit Cards: Most major cards
Personal Checks: Most stores accept checks with proper identification.
Handicapped Accessible: Yes
Food: Castle Garden Cafes Food Court located in mall features a wide variety of eateries.
Bus Tours: Yes, plus bus driver and escort incentives
Notes or Attractions: Built in 1929, the Citadel is a copy of an Assyrian Palace. The Wyndham Garden Hotel is adjacent to mall.

David Textiles Fabric Outlet
5959 Telegraph Road

Directions: Traveling north on the 5 Freeway, exit Washington, turn left on Telegraph, and go approximately ¼ mile. Traveling south on the 5 Freeway, exit Washington, turn left, and go to the first stoplight, which is Telegraph Road. Turn left and go approximately 1 mile.
Phone: (213) 728–3231
Hours: 9:00 A.M.–5:30 P.M., Monday–Saturday; 10:00 A.M.–4:30 P.M., Sunday
Additional Savings: Join the mailing list and receive mailers that announce seasonal sales.
Credit Cards: MasterCard, Visa
Personal Checks: No
Handicapped Accessible: Yes
Food: Within ¼ mile
Bus Tours: Yes

Fabric Outlet
6001 Telegraph Road

Directions: Traveling north on the 5 Freeway, exit Washington and make an immediate left on Telegraph Road. Traveling south on the 5 Freeway, exit Atlantic and turn right. Stay to the right and go over the freeway. Turn right on Telegraph Road.
Phone: (213) 728–1506
Hours: 9:00 A.M.–6:00 P.M., Monday–Saturday; 10:00 A.M.–5:00 P.M., Sunday
Additional Savings: By taking cash only and by not advertising, cost savings are passed on to the customer.
Credit Cards: No
Personal Checks: No
Handicapped Accessible: Yes
Food: Restaurants within walking distance and at The Citadel Outlet Collection
Bus Tours: Yes
Notes or Attractions: Near Citadel Outlet Collection

Cupertino

Spare Changes
10151 De Anza Boulevard

Directions: Call ahead.
Phone: (408) 446–0823
Hours: 11:00 A.M.–7:00 P.M., Monday–Friday; 10:00 A.M.–6:00 P.M., Saturday; 11:00 A.M.–4:00 P.M., Sunday
Additional Savings: Twice-yearly clearance with deep discounts; always a clearance rack with great deals
Credit Cards: MasterCard, Visa
Personal Checks: Yes, with identification
Handicapped Accessible: Yes
Food: Within 1 block

Daly City

Burlington Coat Factory
99 Southgate Avenue

Directions: Call ahead.
Phone: (415) 997–0733
Hours: 9:30 A.M.–9:00 P.M., Monday–Saturday; 11:00 A.M.–6:00 P.M., Sunday
Additional Savings: Warehouse Coat Sale last two weeks of January
Credit Cards: American Express, Discover, MasterCard, Visa
Personal Checks: Yes
Handicapped Accessible: Yes
Food: Westlake Joe's, Nations Hamburgers nearby
Bus Tours: Yes
Notes or Attractions: Five miles from Pacific Ocean beaches

Clothing Clearance Center
2995 Junipero Serra

Directions: South of Market area

Phone: (415) 994–1110
Hours: 10:00 A.M.–8:00 P.M., Monday–Friday; 10:00 A.M.–6:00 P.M., Saturday; noon–5:00 P.M., Sunday
Credit Cards: American Express, Discover, MasterCard, Visa,
Personal Checks: Yes
Handicapped Accessible: Yes
Food: Nearby
Notes or Attractions: Immediate alterations available

Folsom

Natoma Station Factory Outlets
13000 Folsom Boulevard

Directions: Take Highway 50 to Folsom Boulevard exit and turn left.
Phone: (916) 985–0312
Hours: 10:00 A.M.–7:00 P.M., Monday–Wednesday; 10:00 A.M.–9:00 P.M., Thursday–Friday; 10:00 A.M.–6:00 P.M., Saturday; 11:00 A.M.–6:00 P.M., Sunday
Outlets:
Accessorize Fashion Jewelry
Adolfo II
Aileen
American Tourister
Banister Shoes
Barbizon Lingerie
Book Warehouse
Boston Traders
Brass Factory Outlet Store
Bugle Boy
Cape Isle Knitters
Chaus
Corning/Revere
Farberware
Fieldcrest Cannon
Geoffrey Beene
Hawaiian Cotton

Home Again
IYA
Izod
Jones New York
Jordache
Leather Loft
L'eggs/Hanes/Bali
Leslie Fay
Levi's
Natural Footgear
Nike
9 West
Olga/Warner
Omid International Rugs
Perfumania/Fragrance World
The Ribbon Outlet, Inc.
Socks Galore
The Sweatshirt Company
THE Housewares Store
Today's Child
Toy Liquidators
Trend Club
Van Heusen
Wallet Works
Westport Ltd.
Westport Woman
Wicker Factory
Credit Cards: Most major cards
Personal Checks: Most stores accept checks with proper identification.
Handicapped Accessible: Yes
Food: Designer Dogs, Rocky Mountain Chocolate Factory, The Hof Brau, and Top That Yogurt, all located in the mall
Bus Tours: Yes
Notes or Attractions: Near Historic Folsom/Sutter Street, Folsom Lake Recreation Area, Folsom Dam, The American River. Mall style is a Spanish Mission village setting.

Fountain Valley

Krause's Sofa Factory
18370 Pacific Street

Directions: Call ahead.
Phone: (714) 962–8817
Hours: 10:00 A.M.–9:00 P.M., Monday–Friday; 10:00 A.M.–6:00 P.M., Saturday–Sunday
Additional Savings: Semiannual sale (two per year)
Credit Cards: Discover, MasterCard, Visa
Personal Checks: Yes
Handicapped Accessible: Yes
Food: In the vicinity
Bus Tours: No

Fresno

Six Star Factory Outlet
Land Mark Plaza
4027 North Marks

Directions: Call ahead.
Phone: (209) 229–8821
Hours: 9:30 A.M.–8:00 P.M., Monday–Friday; 9:30 A.M.–7:00 P.M., Saturday; 10:00 A.M.–6:00 P.M., Sunday
Credit Cards: MasterCard, Visa
Personal Checks: Yes
Handicapped Accessible: Yes
Food: Available in the vicinity
Bus Tours: Yes

Six Star Factory Outlet
Pak & Save Center
80 East Barstow #103

Directions: Call ahead.
Phone: (209) 431–7689
Hours: 10:00 A.M.–8:00 P.M., Monday–Friday; 11:00 A.M.–7:00 P.M., Saturday; 11:00 A.M.–6:00 P.M., Sunday
Credit Cards: MasterCard, Visa
Personal Checks: Yes
Handicapped Accessible: Yes
Food: Available in the vicinity
Bus Tours: Yes

Six Star Factory Outlet
Fulton Mall
1130 Fulton Mall

Directions: Call ahead.
Phone: (209) 237–3445
Hours: 9:30 A.M.–5:30 P.M., Monday–Saturday; 11:00 A.M.–5:00 P.M., Sunday
Credit Cards: MasterCard, Visa
Personal Checks: Yes
Handicapped Accessible: Yes
Food: Available in the vicinity
Bus Tours: Yes

Fullerton

Catalina
1355 South Harbor Boulevard

Directions: Take 91 Freeway and exit at Harbor Boulevard North.
Phone: (213) 724–4693
Hours: 10:00 A.M.–6:00 P.M., Monday–Thursday; 10:00 A.M.–8:00 P.M., Friday; 10:00 A.M.–5:00 P.M., Saturday; 11:00 A.M.–5:00 P.M., Sunday
Credit Cards: MasterCard, Visa

Personal Checks: Yes (California only)
Handicapped Accessible: Yes
Food: In the vicinity
Bus Tours: Yes

Krause's Sofa Factory
525 North Placentia Avenue

Directions: Call ahead.
Phone: (714) 528–3330
Hours: 10:00 A.M.–9:00 P.M., Monday–Friday; 10:00 A.M.–6:00 P.M., Saturday–Sunday
Additional Savings: Semiannual sale (two per year)
Credit Cards: Discover, MasterCard, Visa
Personal Checks: Yes
Handicapped Accessible: Yes
Food: In the vicinity
Bus Tours: No

Gilroy

Pacific West Outlet Center
8155 Arroyo Circle

Directions: Located off Highway 101 just south of Highway 152
Phone: (408) 847–4155
Hours: 10:00 A.M.–9:00 P.M., Monday–Friday; 9:00 A.M.–9:00 P.M., Saturday; 10:00 A.M.–6:00 P.M., Sunday
Outlets:
Adolfo II
Aileen
Albert Nipon
American Tourister
Anne Klein
Barbizon Lingerie
Bass
Brands

Cape Isle Knitters
Capezio
Carole Hochman Lingerie
Carole Little
Corning/Revere
Crisa
Crystal Works
Eddie Bauer
Famous Brands Housewares
Fila
Fragrance World
Galt Sand
Ganson
Geoffrey Beene
Gitano
Hanes Activewear
harvé benard
He-Ro Group
Home Again
I.B. Diffusion
Iona
Izod
JG Hook
JH Collectibles
Jones New York/Jones Sport
Jordache
Leather Loft
L'eggs/Hanes/Bali
Leon Max
Leslie Fay
Levi's
Liz Claiborne
Maidenform
Mikasa
Nike

9 West
Oneida
Pfaltzgraff
The Ribbon Outlet, Inc.
Sassafras
Sierra Shirts
Shoe Pavilion
Socks Galore
The Sweatshirt Company
Van Heusen
Wallet Works
Wisconsin Toy
Credit Cards: Most major cards
Personal Checks: Most stores accept checks with proper identification.
Handicapped Accessible: Yes
Food: Sensational salads and more at Gilroy Cafe in the mall
Bus Tours: Yes; call (800) 969–3767.
Notes or Attractions: Gilroy is the "garlic capital of the world."

Glendale

Krause's Sofa Factory
115 North Central

Directions: Call ahead.
Phone: (818) 546–1425
Hours: 10:00 A.M.–9:00 P.M., Monday–Friday; 10:00 A.M.–6:00 P.M., Saturday–Sunday
Additional Savings: Semiannual sale (two per year)
Credit Cards: Discover, MasterCard, Visa
Personal Checks: Yes
Handicapped Accessible: Yes
Food: In the vicinity
Bus Tours: No

Hayward

Burlington Coat Factory
1000 La Playa Drive

Directions: Call ahead.
Phone: (510) 782–7073
Hours: 9:30 A.M.–9:00 P.M., Monday–Saturday; 11:00 A.M.–6:00 P.M., Sunday
Additional Savings: Warehouse Coat Sale last two weeks of January
Credit Cards: American Express, Discover, MasterCard, Visa
Personal Checks: Yes
Handicapped Accessible: Yes
Food: A variety of food at the Southland Mall Food Court
Bus Tours: Yes

Huntington Beach

Burlington Coat Factory
7800 Edinger Street

Directions: Call ahead.
Phone: (714) 842–4227
Hours: 10:00 A.M.–9:30 P.M., Monday–Friday; 10:00 A.M.–8:00 P.M., Saturday; 11:00 A.M.–6:00 P.M., Sunday
Additional Savings: Warehouse Coat Sale last two weeks of January
Credit Cards: American Express, Discover, MasterCard, Visa
Personal Checks: Yes
Handicapped Accessible: Yes
Food: Nearby restaurants include Denny's, Marie Calender's, Hof's Hut, and Steakhouse.
Bus Tours: Yes
Notes or Attractions: Near Huntington Center Mall, Sunset Beach, Seal Beach, and Huntington Beach (5 miles)

Sears Outlet
9045 Adams Avenue

Directions: Call ahead.
Phone: (714) 963–2666
Hours: 10:00 A.M.–9:00 P.M., Monday–Friday; 10:00 A.M.–7:00 P.M., Saturday; 11:00 A.M.–6:00 P.M., Sunday
Credit Cards: Discover, Sears
Personal Checks: Yes
Handicapped Accessible: Yes
Food: In the vicinity
Bus Tours: Yes

La Habra

Sears Outlet
1611 West Whittier Boulevard

Directions: Call ahead.
Phone: (310) 694–8500
Hours: 10:00 A.M.–9:00 P.M., Monday–Friday; 10:00 A.M.–7:00 P.M., Saturday; 11:00 A.M.–6:00 P.M., Sunday
Credit Cards: Discover, Sears
Personal Checks: Yes
Handicapped Accessible: Yes
Food: In the vicinity
Bus Tours: Yes

Lake Elsinore

Lake Elsinore Outlet Center
17600 Collier Avenue

Directions: Take I–15 to Central Avenue. Exit and go to Collier Avenue and turn right.
Phone: (714) 245–4989

Hours: 10:00 A.M. – 9:00 P.M., Monday–Saturday; 11:00 A.M.–6:00 P.M., Sunday

Outlets:
Adolfo II
American Tourister
Bass
Cape Isle Knitters
Chicago Cutlery, Etc.
Cole-Haan
Corning/Revere
Famous Brands Housewares
Geoffrey Beene
Gitano
He-Ro Group
i.e.
JH Collectibles
Jones New York
Leather Loft
L'eggs/Hanes/Bali
Leslie Fay
Liz Claiborne
London Fog
Maidenform
Marika
Nathan J. Children's Wear
Nike
9 West
North Face
Oneida
Perfumania
Sbicca Shoes
Socks Galore
Van Heusen
Wallet Works
Welcome Home
Whims-Sarah Coventry Outlet

Credit Cards: Most major cards

Personal Checks: Most stores accept checks with proper identification.

Handicapped Accessible: Yes
Food: Fresh Connection restaurant in mall
Bus Tours: Yes

Lakewood

Bullock's Clearance Center
5005 Clark Avenue

Directions: Call ahead.
Phone: (310) 634–5111
Hours: 10:00 A.M.–9:00 P.M., Monday–Friday; 10:00 A.M.–6:00 P.M., Saturday; noon–6:00 P.M., Sunday
Credit Cards: American Express, MasterCard, Visa
Personal Checks: Yes
Handicapped Accessible: Yes
Food: In the vicinity
Bus Tours: Yes

La Mesa

Bullock's Clearance Center
5500 Grossmont Center Drive

Directions: Call ahead.
Phone: (619) 698–6422
Hours: 10:00 A.M.–9:00 P.M., Monday–Friday; 10:00 A.M.–6:00 P.M., Saturday; 11:00 A.M.–6:00 P.M., Sunday
Credit Cards: American Express, MasterCard, Visa
Personal Checks: Yes
Handicapped Accessible: Yes
Food: In the vicinity
Bus Tours: Yes

La Verne

Catalina
2416 West Foothill Boulevard

Directions: Take 10 Freeway and exit at Garey. Go 5 miles north and make a left at Foothill; located in the Target Shopping Center.
Phone: (714) 593–6415
Hours: 10:00 A.M.–5:00 P.M., Monday–Saturday; 11:00 A.M.–5:00 P.M., Sunday
Credit Cards: MasterCard, Visa
Personal Checks: Yes (California only)
Handicapped Accessible: Yes
Food: In the vicinity
Bus Tours: Yes

Los Angeles

A-1 Furniture Outlet
6002 South Broadway

Directions: Take Harbor Freeway and exit at Gage or Slauson.
Phone: (213) 753–3397 or (213) 758–3963
Hours: By appointment only, Monday–Friday
Credit Cards: No
Personal Checks: Yes
Handicapped Accessible: Yes
Food: Across the street
Bus Tours: Yes
Notes or Attractions: Gardena Gambling Clubs nearby

The Cooper Building
860 South Los Angeles Street

Directions: Located in downtown Los Angeles at Eighth Street and Los Angeles Street
Phone: (213) 622–1139

Hours: 9:30 A.M.–5:30 P.M., Monday–Saturday; 11:00 A.M.–5:00 P.M., Sunday

Outlets:
A&Y Leather Goods
AC Sport
Adler Shoes
Altogether
Athletic Shoe Outlet
Baby Guess?
Betty's Large Sizes
California Girl Dresses
California Sleepwear Outlet
Carus
Casianni
Collectibles
Collectibles Leather
Contempo Collection
Crepe de Chine
Eddy's for Men
Eddy's Men's Shoes
860 Club
Elisabeth Stewart
Eloise
Ernest of California
Eve Hair & Beauty Center
Factory
Fantastic Sportswear
Fantazi Fashions
Fashion Show
For Men Only
Gold Corner
Great Goods
Guess?
Ian Stewart
Judy's Outlet
L.A. Sox
L.A. Style Activewear
Leather Express

Le Club Handbags
Little Folks Outlet
Maurice Shoes
Men at Work
Mom's Gallery Children's Boutique
My Place
Olga/Warner
Paul Stanley Ltd.
Philippe Simon
Salon de Beauté
Scott's Fifth Avenue
Sports Mania Outlet
Tabari Collection
Ticket Sportswear
Unique Jewelry
Windsor Fashions
Credit Cards: Most major cards
Personal Checks: Most stores accept checks with proper identification.
Handicapped Accessible: No
Food: Georgio's Famous Pizza, J&M Gourmet Kitchen, AKW Snack Shop, and Out to Lunch, all in mall
Bus Tours: Yes
Notes or Attractions: Located in L.A.'s Garment District; Daniel Tailor Shop on premises

The Denim Station
852 South Los Angeles Street

Directions: Exit Los Angeles Street from 10 Freeway in downtown Los Angeles. Exit Ninth Street from 110 Freeway. Exit Los Angeles Street from 101 Freeway.
Phone: (213) 627–1758
Hours: 9:30 A.M.–6:00 P.M., Monday–Saturday
Additional Savings: Seasonal sales and special sales
Credit Cards: American Express, Discover, MasterCard, Visa; ATM
Personal Checks: Yes
Handicapped Accessible: Yes

Food: In the immediate area, food court includes twenty different restaurants with a wide variety of food.
Bus Tours: Yes
Notes or Attractions: Cooper Building, California Mart, museum, zoo, and historical landmarks all nearby

The Framing Center
8301 West Third Street

Directions: Call ahead.
Phone: (213) 655–1296
Hours: 10:00 A.M.–6:00 P.M., Monday–Saturday
Additional Savings: March–April, summer, and Christmas sales
Credit Cards: MasterCard, Visa
Personal Checks: Yes
Handicapped Accessible: Yes
Food: One block away
Bus Tours: Yes
Notes or Attractions: Near Beverly Center Mall and Hard Rock Cafe

Krause's Sofa Factory
9830 West Pico Boulevard

Directions: Call ahead.
Phone: (310) 277–5946
Hours: 10:00 A.M.–9:00 P.M., Monday–Friday; 10:00 A.M.–6:00 P.M., Saturday–Sunday
Additional Savings: Semiannual sale (two per year)
Credit Cards: Discover, MasterCard, Visa
Personal Checks: Yes
Handicapped Accessible: Yes
Food: In the vicinity
Bus Tours: No

Los Banos

Six Star Factory Outlet
National Shopping Center
1237 Pacheco Boulevard

Directions: Call ahead.
Phone: (209) 626–0581
Hours: 9:30 A.M.–7:00 P.M., Monday–Thursday; 9:30 A.M.–8:00 P.M., Friday; 10:00 A.M.–6:00 P.M., Saturday
Credit Cards: MasterCard, Visa
Personal Checks: Yes
Handicapped Accessible: Yes
Food: Available in the vicinity
Bus Tours: Yes

Madera

Six Star Factory Outlet
300 East Yosemite Avenue

Directions: Located in downtown Madera
Phone: (209) 674–9410
Hours: 9:30 A.M.–7:00 P.M., Monday–Saturday; 10:00 A.M.–6:00 P.M., Sunday
Credit Cards: MasterCard, Visa
Personal Checks: Yes
Handicapped Accessible: Yes
Food: Available in the vicinity
Bus Tours: Yes

Mammoth Lakes

Mammoth Factory Stores
3343 Main Street

Directions: Call ahead.

Phone: (619) 934–7040
Hours: 10:00 A.M.–6:00 P.M., Monday–Thursday; 10:00 A.M.–8:00 P.M., Friday–Saturday; 10:00 A.M.–6:00 P.M., Sunday
Outlets:
Adrienne Vittadini
Bass
Book Warehouse
Geoffrey Beene
Polo/Ralph Lauren
Van Heusen
Credit Cards: Most major cards
Personal Checks: Most stores accept checks with proper identification.
Handicapped Accessible: Yes
Food: Delicatessen and Italian Cafe in mall
Bus Tours: Yes
Notes or Attractions: Skiing nearby; ski shops in mall

Marina

Six Star Factory Outlet
Sea Crest Plaza
272 Reservation Road

Directions: Call ahead.
Phone: (408) 384–1402
Hours: 10:00 A.M.–9:00 P.M., Monday–Friday; 10:00 A.M.–8:00 P.M., Saturday–Sunday
Credit Cards: MasterCard, Visa
Personal Checks: Yes
Handicapped Accessible: Yes
Food: Available in the vicinity
Bus Tours: Yes

Milpitas

Six Star Factory Outlet
Park Victoria Plaza
30 South Park Victoria Drive

Directions: Call ahead.
Phone: (408) 945–8388
Hours: 10:00 A.M.–8:00 P.M., Monday–Friday; 10:00 A.M.–7:00 P.M., Saturday; 10:00 A.M.–6:00 P.M., Sunday
Credit Cards: MasterCard, Visa
Personal Checks: Yes
Handicapped Accessible: Yes
Food: Available in the vicinity
Bus Tours: Yes

Modesto

Royal Robbins
1508 Tenth Street

Directions: At the corner of Needham and Tenth Street in downtown Modesto
Phone: (209) 522–3500
Hours: 10:00 A.M.–6:00 P.M., Monday–Friday; 10:00 A.M.–5:00 P.M., Saturday; noon–4:00 P.M., Sunday
Credit Cards: MasterCard, Visa
Personal Checks: Yes
Handicapped Accessible: Yes
Food: Nearby
Bus Tours: No
Notes or Attractions: Major shopping mecca for bargain hunters; many factory outlets nearby

Monrovia

Krause's Sofa Factory
622 West Huntington Drive

Directions: Call ahead.
Phone: (818) 303–3661
Hours: 10:00 A.M.–9:00 P.M., Monday–Friday; 10:00 A.M.–6:00 P.M., Saturday–Sunday
Additional Savings: Semiannual sale (two per year)
Credit Cards: Discover, MasterCard, Visa
Personal Checks: Yes
Handicapped Accessible: Yes
Food: In the vicinity
Bus Tours: No

National City

Upholstery Fabric Outlet (UFO)
1918 Roosevelt Avenue

Directions: Take I–5 and exit Twenty-fourth Street East to Hoover; turn left and go a few blocks to a dead end. At the dead end, there will be a sign saying UFO and an arrow pointing to the right, which leads to the parking lot.
Phone: (619) 477–9341
Hours: 9:00 A.M.–5:30 P.M., Monday–Saturday
Credit Cards: MasterCard, Visa
Personal Checks: Yes
Handicapped Accessible: Yes
Food: A number of restaurants within five- to ten-minute drive
Bus Tours: Yes
Notes or Attractions: Located just south of San Diego; Mexico is another fifteen-minute drive south.

Newbury Park

Krause's Sofa Factory
2810 Camino Dos Rios

Directions: Call ahead.
Phone: (805) 499–6734
Hours: 10:00 A.M.–9:00 P.M., Monday–Friday; 10:00 A.M.–6:00 P.M., Saturday–Sunday
Additional Savings: Semiannual sale (two per year)
Credit Cards: Discover, MasterCard, Visa
Personal Checks: Yes
Handicapped Accessible: Yes
Food: In the vicinity
Bus Tours: No

Northridge

Catalina
9040 Balboa Boulevard

Directions: Take 405 Freeway and exit at Nordhoff. Go east to Balboa; located on the corner.
Phone: (818) 894–3422
Hours: 10:00 A.M.–5:00 P.M., Monday–Saturday; 11:00 A.M.–5:00 P.M., Sunday
Credit Cards: MasterCard, Visa
Personal Checks: Yes (California only)
Handicapped Accessible: Yes
Food: In the vicinity
Bus Tours: Yes

Norwalk

Sears Outlet
13927 Pioneer Boulevard

Directions: Call ahead.
Phone: (310) 864–7761
Hours: 10:00 A.M.–9:00 P.M., Monday–Friday; 10:00 A.M.–7:00 P.M., Saturday; 10:00 A.M.–6:00 P.M., Sunday
Credit Cards: Discover, Sears
Personal Checks: Yes
Handicapped Accessible: Yes
Food: In the vicinity
Bus Tours: Yes

Oakland

Malson's Ragsmatazz
2021 Broadway

Directions: Call ahead.
Phone: (510) 495–5037
Hours: 10:00 A.M.–6:00 P.M., Monday–Saturday
Credit Cards: MasterCard, Visa
Personal Checks: Yes, with driver's license (no post-office-box addresses on checks)
Handicapped Accessible: Yes
Food: A few restaurants nearby
Bus Tours: Yes
Notes or Attractions: Near The Paramount Theater and Jack London Square

Ontario

Plaza Continental Factory Stores
3700 East Inland Empire Boulevard

Directions: Exit I–10 at Haven to Inland Empire Boulevard; just five minutes from the Ontario airport.
Phone: (714) 980–6231
Hours: 10:00 A.M.–9:00 P.M., Monday–Saturday; 10:00 A.M.–6:00 P.M., Sunday
Outlets:
Adolfo II
Aileen
Book Warehouse
Capezio
Converse
Corning/Revere
Crisa
Gitano
Hathaway
In 2 Shape/Designer's Own
Leather Loft
Olga/Warner
Prestige Fragrance & Cosmetics
Sbicca Shoes
Welcome Home
Whims-Sarah Coventry Outlet
Credit Cards: Most major cards
Personal Checks: Most stores accept checks with proper identification.
Handicapped Accessible: Yes
Food: El Torito, Black Angus, and Spoons Bar & Grill in the mall
Bus Tours: Yes

Pacifica

Six Star Factory Outlet
Fairmont Shopping Center

787 Hickey Boulevard
Directions: Call ahead.
Phone: (415) 359–4120
Hours: 9:30 A.M.–9:00 P.M., Monday–Saturday; 10:00 A.M.–7:00 P.M., Sunday
Credit Cards: MasterCard, Visa
Personal Checks: Yes
Handicapped Accessible: Yes
Food: Available in the vicinity
Bus Tours: Yes

Pacific Grove

American Tin Cannery Outlet Center
125 Ocean View Boulevard

Directions: Take Scenic Route 1 to the Pacific Grove exit. Follow the signs to Cannery Row and Aquarium. Outlet center is 1 block past the aquarium on Ocean View Boulevard.
Phone: (408) 372–1442
Hours: 10:00 A.M.–6:00 P.M., Monday–Wednesday; 10:00 A.M.–9:00 P.M., Thursday–Friday; 10:00 A.M.–6:00 P.M., Saturday; 11:00 A.M.–5:00 P.M., Sunday
Outlets:
Aca Joe
Aileen
Banister Shoes
Barbie Store
Barbizon Lingerie
Bass
Book Warehouse
Brass Factory Outlet Store

Cape Isle Knitters
Carole Little
Carter's Childrenswear
Corning/Revere
Dynasty Imports
Geoffrey Beene
Gitano
Hanes Activewear
Home Again
Joan & David Designer Outlet
Leather Loft
L'eggs/Hanes/Bali
Maidenform
Mattel Toy Club
Oneida
PFC Fragrance & Cosmetics
Polly Flinders
The Ribbon Outlet, Inc.
Royal Doulton
Royal House
Sunglass World
THE Housewares Store
totes Factory Stores
Van Heusen
Wallet Works
Westport Ltd.
Westport Woman
Whims-Sarah Coventry Outlet
Women's Fashions
Credit Cards: Most major cards
Personal Checks: Most stores accept checks with proper identification.
Handicapped Accessible: Yes
Food: A wide variety of restaurants are located in the mall.
Bus Tours: Yes
Notes or Attractions: On the spectacular Monterey Peninsula near famous Cannery Row, Monterey Bay Aquarium, Wax Museum, Fisherman's Wharf, Pacific Grove Museum of Natural History, The 17-Mile Drive and Pebble Beach

Palo Alto

North Face Factory Outlet
217 Alma Street

Directions: From Highway 280, take Page Mill East across the El Camino. Second right is Alma Street. Go north 3 miles; store is on the right. From Highway 101, take University Street West exit through downtown Palo Alto. Take a right on Alma Street; store is 3 blocks on the right.
Phone: (415) 325–3231
Hours: 10:00 A.M.–8:00 P.M., Monday–Thursday; 10:00 A.M.–6:00 P.M., Friday–Saturday; 11:00 A.M.–5:00 P.M., Sunday
Additional Savings: End-of-the-year clearance, 30 to 70 percent off
Credit Cards: American Express, Discover, MasterCard, Visa
Personal Checks: Yes
Handicapped Accessible: Yes
Food: University Avenue has about a dozen restaurants that range from cafeteria style to four-star eateries.
Bus Tours: No
Notes or Attractions: Stanford University is across the street.

Pismo Beach

London Fog
533 Five Cities Drive

Directions: From Los Angeles, take 101 North to Pismo Beach, exit at Fourth Street. From San Francisco, take 101 South to Pismo Beach and exit at Fourth Street.
Phone: (805) 773–5755
Hours: 9:30 A.M.–7:00 P.M., Monday–Friday; 9:30 A.M.–6:00 P.M., Saturday; 10:00 A.M.–6:00 P.M., Sunday (subject to change)
Credit Cards: Discover, MasterCard, Visa
Personal Checks: Yes, with two forms of identification
Handicapped Accessible: No
Food: Across the street

Bus Tours: Yes
Notes or Attractions: Hearst Castle (45 miles north) and Solvang (45 miles south)

Pittsburg

Burlington Coat Factory
Century Plaza Shopping Center

Directions: Call ahead.
Phone: (510) 778–3398
Hours: 9:30 A.M.–8:00 P.M., Monday–Saturday; 11:00 A.M.–6:00 P.M., Sunday
Additional Savings: Warehouse Coat Sale last two weeks of January
Credit Cards: American Express, Discover, MasterCard, Visa
Personal Checks: Yes
Handicapped Accessible: Yes
Food: Ten restaurants within 1 mile
Bus Tours: Yes
Notes or Attractions: Sacramento Delta (swimming and waterskiing)

Rancho Cordova

Six Star Factory Outlet
Mills Center
10371 Folsom Boulevard

Directions: Call ahead.
Phone: (916) 361–3474
Hours: 10:00 A.M.–8:00 P.M., Monday–Friday; 10:00 A.M.–6:00 P.M., Saturday; 11:00 A.M.–5:00 P.M., Sunday
Credit Cards: MasterCard, Visa
Personal Checks: Yes
Handicapped Accessible: Yes
Food: Available in the vicinity
Bus Tours: Yes

Riverside

Catalina
5232 Arlington Avenue

Directions: Take 91 Freeway and exit at Madison. Go west three stop-lights to Arlington and then go south.
Phone: (714) 688–1660
Hours: 10:00 A.M.–6:00 P.M., Monday–Friday; 10:00 A.M.–5:00 P.M., Saturday; 11:00 A.M.–5:00 P.M., Sunday
Credit Cards: MasterCard, Visa
Personal Checks: Yes (California only)
Handicapped Accessible: Yes
Food: In the vicinity
Bus Tours: Yes

Rowland Heights

Catalina
19722 East Colima Road

Directions: Take 60 Freeway and exit Fairway. Go south to Colima Road; located at Stater Brothers Shopping Center.
Phone: (714) 598–3802
Hours: 9:00 A.M.–5:00 P.M., Monday–Saturday; 11:00 A.M.–5:00 P.M., Sunday
Credit Cards: MasterCard, Visa
Personal Checks: Yes (California only)
Handicapped Accessible: Yes
Food: In the vicinity
Bus Tours: Yes

Sacramento

Six Star Factory Outlet
Stockridge Shopping Center
5025 Fruitridge Boulevard

Directions: Call ahead.
Phone: (916) 455–7827
Hours: 10:00 A.M.–8:00 P.M., Monday–Friday; 10:00 A.M.–6:00 P.M., Saturday; 11:00 A.M.–6:00 P.M., Sunday
Credit Cards: MasterCard, Visa
Personal Checks: Yes
Handicapped Accessible: Yes
Food: Available in the vicinity
Bus Tours: Yes

Six Star Factory Outlet
Valley Mack Plaza
6234 Mack Road

Directions: Call ahead.
Phone: (916) 422–7827
Hours: 10:00 A.M.–8:00 P.M., Monday–Friday; 10:00 A.M.–6:00 P.M., Saturday–Sunday
Credit Cards: MasterCard, Visa
Personal Checks: Yes
Handicapped Accessible: Yes
Food: Available in the vicinity
Bus Tours: Yes

St. Helena

Home Again
801 Main Street

Directions: Call ahead.
Phone: (707) 963–8163

Hours: 10:00 A.M.–6:00 P.M., Monday–Sunday
Credit Cards: American Express, Discover, MasterCard, Visa
Personal Checks: Yes
Handicapped Accessible: Yes
Food: Nearby
Bus Tours: Yes

Salinas

Six Star Factory Outlet
Alisal Shopping Center
876 East Alisal Street

Directions: Call ahead.
Phone: (408) 754–2833
Hours: 10:00 A.M.–6:45 P.M., Monday–Thursday; 10:00 A.M.–7:45 P.M., Friday; 11:00 A.M.–6:45 P.M., Saturday–Sunday
Credit Cards: MasterCard, Visa
Personal Checks: Yes
Handicapped Accessible: Yes
Food: Available in the vicinity
Bus Tours: Yes

Sand City

Couroc
1725 Contra Costa

Directions: From Highway 1, take exit for Highway 218 (Seaside, Del Rey Oaks); at first set of traffic lights, turn left onto Del Monte Boulevard; at the second set of traffic lights, turn left onto Contra Costa. From Freemont Boulevard, turn onto Broadway and head toward the ocean; turn right at Del Monte Boulevard and make a quick left onto Contra Costa. From downtown Monterey, take Del Monte Avenue going north; go past the Days Inn and turn left onto Contra Costa (third set of lights after Days Inn).
Phone: (408) 394–3511

Hours: 10:00 A.M.–5:00 P.M., Monday–Saturday; noon–5:00 P.M., Sunday
Additional Savings: Additional sales are based on daily and weekly production.
Credit Cards: American Express, Diners Club, Discover, JCB, MasterCard, Visa
Personal Checks: Yes
Handicapped Accessible: Yes
Food: Within ½ mile
Bus Tours: Yes
Notes or Attractions: All the attractions of the Monterey Peninsula (Carmel, Pebble Beach, Monterey, Pacific Grove) are within minutes of the store.

San Diego

Apparel Designer Zone
6663 El Cajon Boulevard

Directions: Call ahead.
Phone: (619) 460–4370
Hours: 11:00 A.M.–8:00 P.M., Monday–Friday; 11:00 A.M.–6:00 P.M., Saturday–Sunday
Additional Savings: Various sales throughout the year
Credit Cards: American Express, MasterCard, Visa
Personal Checks: Yes
Handicapped Accessible: Yes
Food: Within ¼ mile
Bus Tours: No
Notes or Attractions: Nightclubs and food establishments nearby

Apparel Designer Zone
931 Garnet Avenue

Directions: Call ahead.
Phone: (619) 483–5150
Hours: 11:00 A.M.–9:00 P.M., Monday–Friday; 11:00 A.M.–6:00 P.M., Saturday–Sunday

Additional Savings: Various sales throughout the year
Credit Cards: American Express, MasterCard, Visa
Personal Checks: Yes
Handicapped Accessible: Yes
Food: Within ¼ mile
Bus Tours: No
Notes or Attractions: Nightclubs and food establishments nearby

Apparel Designer Zone
8250 Camino Santa Fe

Directions: Call ahead.
Phone: (619) 450–3323
Hours: 11:00 A.M.–8:00 P.M., Monday–Friday; 11:00 A.M.–6:00 P.M., Saturday–Sunday
Additional Savings: Various sales throughout the year
Credit Cards: American Express, MasterCard, Visa
Personal Checks: Yes
Handicapped Accessible: Yes
Food: Within ¼ mile
Bus Tours: No
Notes or Attractions: Nightclubs and food establishments nearby

Discount Fabrics
3325 Adams Avenue

Directions: Take I–805 to Adams Avenue East to store in old Adams Avenue movie theater.
Phone: (619) 280–1791
Hours: 10:00 A.M.–5:30 P.M., Monday–Friday; 10:00 A.M.–5:00 P.M., Saturday
Credit Cards: MasterCard, Visa
Personal Checks: San Diego area only
Handicapped Accessible: Yes
Food: Restaurants nearby
Bus Tours: Yes

Nordstrom Rack
824 Camino del Rio North

Directions: Call ahead.
Phone: (619) 296–0143
Hours: 9:30 A.M.–9:30 P.M., Monday–Friday; 9:30 A.M.–7:00 P.M., Saturday; 11:00 A.M.–6:00 P.M., Sunday
Additional Savings: Legendary 25-percent and 50-percent off sales
Credit Cards: American Express, MasterCard, Nordstrom, Visa
Personal Checks: Yes, with two forms of identification
Handicapped Accessible: Yes
Food: Nearby
Bus Tours: Yes; call ahead for information.

Sears Outlet
3450 College Avenue

Directions: Call ahead.
Phone: (619) 583–9802
Hours: 10:00 A.M.–9:00 P.M., Monday–Friday; 10:00 A.M.–7:00 P.M., Saturday; 10:00 A.M.–6:00 P.M., Sunday
Credit Cards: Discover, Sears
Personal Checks: Yes
Handicapped Accessible: Yes
Food: In the vicinity
Bus Tours: Yes

San Dimas

Krause's Sofa Factory
150 Village Court

Directions: Take 10 Freeway to 210 Pasadena Freeway; exit Arrow Highway San Dimas. Take a right off the freeway to first light; then take a left at first light (Village Court).
Phone: (714) 599–9376
Hours: 10:00 A.M.–9:00 P.M., Monday–Friday; 10:00 A.M.–6:00 P.M., Saturday–Sunday

Additional Savings: Semiannual sale (two per year); 10-percent discount plus free sales tax; buy sofa and loveseat and get a free chair or recliner.
Credit Cards: Discover, MasterCard, Visa
Personal Checks: Yes
Handicapped Accessible: Yes
Food: Sizzler and McDonald's right across the street
Bus Tours: No
Notes or Attractions: Near Raging Waters, Pinelli Park, Puddingstone Lake

San Francisco

Aca Joe
148 Townsend Street

Directions: South of Market Street
Phone: (415) 541–9192
Hours: 10:00 A.M.–5:30 P.M., Monday–Friday; 9:00 A.M.–5:30 P.M., Saturday; noon–4:30 P.M., Sunday
Credit Cards: American Express, Discover, MasterCard, Visa
Personal Checks: Yes
Handicapped Accessible: Yes
Food: Within minutes
Bus Tours: Yes

AHC Apparel/Go Silk
625 Second Street

Directions: South of Market area
Phone: (415) 957–1983
Hours: 10:00 A.M.–5:00 P.M., Monday–Saturday
Credit Cards: American Express, MasterCard, Visa
Personal Checks: Yes, with identification
Handicapped Accessible: Yes
Food: Nearby

Alley Kat
45 Stanford Street

Directions: Take 101 South toward Bay Bridge; exit at Sixth Street. Head east to Brannan; turn left and go past Third Street. At the first street on the right, turn right—this is Stanford. The store is in the middle of the block.
Phone: (415) 512–9570
Hours: 10:00 A.M.–5:00 P.M., Monday–Friday; 9:00 A.M.–5:00 P.M., Saturday; 11:00 A.M.–5:00 P.M., Sunday
Credit Cards: No
Personal Checks: Yes
Handicapped Accessible: No
Food: One and a half short blocks away
Bus Tours: Yes
Notes or Attractions: Located in the heart of the outlet stores; close to Pier 39, Fisherman's Wharf, and Union Square

ASAP Athletic Shoe Outlet
899 Howard Street

Directions: South of Market area
Phone: (415) 495–2483
Hours: 9:30 A.M.–6:00 P.M., Monday–Saturday; noon–5:00 P.M., Sunday
Credit Cards: American Express, MasterCard, Visa
Personal Checks: Yes
Handicapped Accessible: Yes
Food: Within 1 block
Bus Tours: Yes

A Shopping Spree
180 Townsend Street

Directions: Take 101 South and exit at Fourth Street. Go 2 blocks and turn left on Townsend. Store is located between Second and Third streets.
Phone: (415) 495–7385

Hours: 11:00 A.M.–5:00 P.M., Monday–Friday; 10:00 A.M.–5:00 P.M., Saturday; closed Sunday
Additional Savings: Discount coupon in "South of Market Outlet Guide"; additional discount on volume purchase
Credit Cards: MasterCard, Visa ($15 minimum)
Personal Checks: Local personalized checks only, with current driver's license and major credit card (as a credit reference)
Handicapped Accessible: No
Food: Restaurants a half-block away
Bus Tours: Yes
Notes or Attractions: Located in the outlet area and close to Convention Center and many hotels

Bali Importers Outlet
899 Howard Street, Suite 111

Directions: Call ahead.
Phone: (415) 896–9619
Hours: 10:00 A.M.–9:00 P.M., Monday–Sunday
Credit Cards: MasterCard, Visa
Personal Checks: Yes
Handicapped Accessible: Yes
Food: Within walking distance
Bus Tours: Yes

Basic Brown Bear Factory and Store
444 Dehard Street

Directions: Call ahead.
Phone: (415) 626–0781
Hours: 10:00 A.M.–5:00 P.M., Monday–Saturday; 1:00 P.M.–5:00 P.M., Sunday
Credit Cards: American Express, MasterCard, Visa
Personal Checks: Yes
Handicapped Accessible: Only to the first level for wheelchairs
Food: Restaurants within walking distance. A pizza parlor and an ice-cream parlor are two minutes away by car.

Bus Tours: Yes
Notes or Attractions: Drop-in tours: Monday–Friday at 1:00 P.M. and 2:00 P.M.; Saturdays at 11:00 A.M. and 2:00 P.M.; Sundays at 3:00 P.M.. Five minutes away from the Esprit outlet and ten minutes away from Aca Joe and Gunne Sax outlets.

Bridal Discount Outlet
300 Brannan Street

Directions: South of Market area
Phone: (415) 495–7922
Hours: 10:00 A.M.–5:00 P.M., Monday–Saturday; 11:00 A.M.–5:00 P.M., Sunday
Credit Cards: MasterCard, Visa
Personal Checks: Only for deposits
Handicapped Accessible: Yes
Food: Nearby

Bridal Veil Outlet
124 Spear Street

Directions: South of Market area
Phone: (415) 495–7922
Hours: 10:00 A.M.–4:00 P.M., Monday–Saturday
Credit Cards: MasterCard, Visa
Personal Checks: Only for deposits
Handicapped Accessible: Yes
Food: Nearby

Burlington Coat Factory
899 Howard Street

Directions: Call ahead.
Phone: (415) 495–7234
Hours: 9:30 A.M.–8:00 P.M., Monday–Saturday; 11:00 A.M.–6:00 P.M., Sunday

Additional Savings: Warehouse Coat Sale last two weeks of January
Credit Cards: American Express, Discover, MasterCard, Visa
Personal Checks: Yes
Handicapped Accessible: Yes
Food: M&M Bar & Grill, Chevy's Mexican Restaurant, Cadillac Bar, Strawberry's Cafe—all nearby
Bus Tours: Yes
Notes or Attractions: Near Cable Cars, Fisherman's Wharf, Coit Tower, Union Square

Byer Factory Outlet
1300 Bryant Street

Directions: South of Market area
Phone: (415) 626–1228
Hours: 10:00 A.M.–5:00 P.M., Friday–Saturday
Credit Cards: MasterCard, Visa
Personal Checks: Yes, with driver's license
Handicapped Accessible: Yes
Food: Nearby

Capricorn Coffees
353 Tenth Street

Directions: South of Market area
Phone: (415) 621–8500
Hours: 8:30 A.M.–5:30 P.M., Monday–Friday; 10:00 A.M.–2:00 P.M., Saturday
Credit Cards: MasterCard, Visa
Personal Checks: Yes
Handicapped Accessible: Yes
Food: Nearby

Clothing Clearance Center
510 Bryant Street

Directions: South of Market area
Phone: (415) 495–7879
Hours: 10:00 A.M.–7:00 P.M., Monday–Friday; 10:00 A.M.–6:00 P.M., Saturday; 11:00 A.M.–5:00 P.M., Sunday
Credit Cards: American Express, Discover, MasterCard, Visa
Personal Checks: Yes
Handicapped Accessible: Yes
Food: Nearby
Notes or Attractions: Immediate alterations available

Comfort Connection
1295 Folsom Street

Directions: South of Market area
Phone: (415) 861–3182
Hours: 10:00 A.M.–6:00 P.M., Monday–Tuesday, Friday–Saturday; 10:00 A.M.–7:00 P.M., Wednesday–Thursday; 11:00 A.M.–5:00 P.M., Sunday
Credit Cards: American Express, Discover, MasterCard, Visa
Personal Checks: Yes
Handicapped Accessible: Yes
Food: Nearby
Notes or Attractions: Financing available

Déjà Vu à Paris
400 Brannan Street

Directions: South of Market area
Phone: (415) 541–9177
Hours: 11:00 A.M.–5:00 P.M., Monday–Friday; 10:00 A.M.–5:00 P.M., Saturday
Credit Cards: American Express, MasterCard, Visa
Personal Checks: Yes
Handicapped Accessible: Yes
Food: Nearby

Designers' Outlet
300 Brannan Street/Suite 102

Directions: South of Market area
Phone: (415) 957–5978
Hours: 10:00 A.M.–5:00 P.M., Monday–Saturday; 11:30 A.M.–4:30 P.M.,
Sunday
Credit Cards: MasterCard, Visa
Personal Checks: Yes
Handicapped Accessible: Yes
Food: Within walking distance
Bus Tours: Yes
Notes or Attractions: Gunne Sax a half-block away

East West Concepts
510 Bryant Street

Directions: South of Market area
Phone: (415) 777–5918
Hours: 10:00 A.M.–6:00 P.M., Monday–Saturday
Credit Cards: American Express, MasterCard, Visa
Personal Checks: Yes
Handicapped Accessible: Yes
Food: Nearby

Eileen West Outlet
2915 Sacramento Street

Directions: From South Bay/East Bay, take 101 Freeway to Van Ness
exit; follow Van Ness north and turn left on Geary Boulevard; make a
left on Divisidero and another left on Sacramento Street. From North
Bay, cross the Golden Gate Bridge and go to Lombard Street; turn right
on Divisidero and then right on Sacramento.
Phone: (415) 563–0113
Hours: 10:00 A.M.–6:00 P.M., Monday–Saturday; noon–5:00 P.M., Sunday
Additional Savings: Three to four seasonal sales; fill out card in store to
be put on mailing list.

Credit Cards: MasterCard, Visa
Personal Checks: Yes
Handicapped Accessible: Yes
Food: Great coffee cafe around the corner; also many restaurants on Sacramento and Fillmore streets 2-3 blocks away
Bus Tours: No
Notes or Attractions: More great shops farther up on Sacramento Street

End of the Line
275 Brannan Street

Directions: Located in the South of Market district
Phone: (415) 989–0234
Hours: 10:00 A.M.–5:00 P.M., Monday–Friday; 9:30 A.M.–5:00 P.M., Saturday
Additional Savings: Discount coupons in various bus-tour books
Credit Cards: Discover, MasterCard, Visa
Personal Checks: Yes
Handicapped Accessible: No
Food: A fabulous sandwich shop and espresso bar nearby
Bus Tours: Yes
Notes or Attractions: Fisherman's Wharf, Pier 39, Aquatic Park, Union Square, Moscone Center all nearby

Esprit
499 Illinois Street

Directions: At Sixteenth Street and Illinois Street
Phone: (415) 957–2540
Hours: 10:00 A.M.–8:00 P.M., Monday–Friday; 10:00 A.M.–7:00 P.M., Saturday; 11:00 A.M.–5:00 P.M., Sunday
Additional Savings: Sign up at register for mailing list to receive sale announcements.
Credit Cards: American Express, MasterCard, Visa
Personal Checks: Yes
Handicapped Accessible: Yes

Food: Caffe Esprit, adjacent to the store, is open 11:30 A.M.–3:00 P.M. Monday–Saturday.
Bus Tours: Yes
Notes or Attractions: Many other outlets within a five-minute drive

Fashion Bin
615 Third Street

Directions: South of Market area between Townsend and Brannan
Phone: (415) 495–2264
Hours: 10:00 A.M.–5:00 P.M., Monday–Saturday
Additional Savings: Up to 75 percent off in January
Credit Cards: MasterCard, Visa
Personal Checks: No
Handicapped Accessible: Yes
Food: Nearby
Bus Tours: Yes
Notes or Attractions: Flower Mart, Cartoon Museum, San Francisco train station all nearby

Fashion Intuitions
679 Third Street

Directions: South of Market area on Third Street between Townsend and Brannan
Phone: (415) 495–4310
Hours: 9:30 A.M.–5:30 P.M., Monday–Saturday
Additional Savings: Christmas, preseason, Labor Day, and spring clearance sales
Credit Cards: Carte Blanche, Diners Club, JCB, MasterCard, Visa
Personal Checks: Yes
Handicapped Accessible: Yes
Food: Many restaurants within the block
Bus Tours: Yes
Notes or Attractions: Near Union Square, Fisherman's Wharf, other outlets

$5 & $10 Store for Women
899 Howard Street

Directions: Call ahead.
Phone: (415) 546–1893
Hours: 10:00 A.M.–9:00 P.M., Monday–Sunday
Credit Cards: MasterCard, Visa
Personal Checks: Yes
Handicapped Accessible: Yes
Food: Within walking distance
Bus Tours: Yes

Four Star Apparel Company
625 Second Street

Directions: South of Market area
Phone: (415) 512–8212
Hours: 10:00 A.M.–4:00 P.M., Monday–Friday; 10:00 A.M.–5:00 P.M., Saturday
Credit Cards: MasterCard, Visa
Personal Checks: Yes
Handicapped Accessible: Yes
Food: Nearby

Fritzi Outlet
218 Fremont Street

Directions: Take Freemont Street exit off Bay Bridge heading west. Take the same exit heading north on Highway 101 toward Bay Bridge.
Phone: (415) 979–1399
Hours: 9:00 A.M.–5:00 P.M., Monday–Thursday; 8:00 A.M.–5:00 P.M., Friday–Saturday
Additional Savings: Early Bird Sale 8:00 A.M.–10:00 A.M. Friday. Shop on your birthday for 20 percent discount off nonsale items (identification required).
Credit Cards: Discover, MasterCard, Visa ($10 minimum)
Personal Checks: Yes, with identification ($10 minimum)

Handicapped Accessible: Yes
Food: Within 1 block
Bus Tours: Yes

Georgiou Outlet
925 Bryant Street

Directions: From downtown take Eighth Street to Bryant Street; turn left, then right on Langton for parking.
Phone: (415) 554–0150
Hours: Call ahead for current hours.
Credit Cards: American Express, Discover, MasterCard, Visa
Personal Checks: Yes
Handicapped Accessible: Yes
Food: Two-block walk
Bus Tours: Yes

Golden Rainbow Outlet
435 Brannan Street

Directions: South of Market area between Third and Fourth streets on Brannan
Phone: (415) 543–5191
Hours: Noon–5:00 P.M., Tuesday–Friday; 10:00 A.M.–5:00 P.M., Saturday
Additional Savings: Fifty-percent sale for two weeks in January and August
Credit Cards: MasterCard, Visa
Personal Checks: Yes
Handicapped Accessible: Yes
Food: A half-block away
Bus Tours: No
Notes or Attractions: Other outlet stores nearby

Gunne Sax Outlet
35 Stanford Street

Directions: Off Brannan Street between Second and Third streets
Phone: (415) 495–3327
Hours: 10:00 A.M.–5:00 P.M., Monday–Friday; 9:00 A.M.–5:00 P.M., Saturday; 11:00 A.M.–5:00 P.M., Sunday
Additional Savings: Four sales a year with markdowns of 30 to 40 percent off already low outlet prices
Credit Cards: American Express, MasterCard, Visa
Personal Checks: Yes
Handicapped Accessible: Yes
Food: Within 1 block
Bus Tours: Yes

Happy Times Jewelry
665 Third Street

Directions: Take 101 North to 80 East, exit on Fourth Street, and go 2 blocks to Townsend. Turn left and left again on Third Street. From Bay Bridge, exit at Fifth Street, turn right and go to Fourth Street. Turn right, go to Townsend, turn left and left again on Third Street.
Phone: (415) 495–7545
Hours: 10:00 A.M.–5:30 P.M., Monday–Saturday; noon–4:00 P.M., some Sundays (call ahead)
Additional Savings: At the end of each season, there is an additional savings on fashion jewelry. A storewide sale is held the week after Christmas.
Credit Cards: American Express, MasterCard, Visa
Personal Checks: Yes (California only)
Handicapped Accessible: Yes
Food: Within 1 block
Bus Tours: Street parking only
Notes or Attractions: Numerous other outlets in the area

Image Fashion
899 Howard Street, #109

Directions: One block from Moscone Center; 2 blocks south of Market Street at the corner of Fifth Street and Howard Street.
Phone: (415) 512–8785
Hours: 10:00 A.M.–6:00 P.M., Monday–Saturday; 11:00 A.M.–5:00 P.M., Sunday
Additional Savings: Clearance sales and seasonal sales
Credit Cards: American Express, Discover, MasterCard, Visa
Personal Checks: Yes
Handicapped Accessible: Yes
Food: Next door and 1 block away
Bus Tours: Yes
Notes or Attractions: Shoe stores, toy store, accessory store, and cafe nearby

In Jewels
899 Howard Street, #108

Directions: At the corner of Fifth Street and Howard Street; Muni and cable cars 1-2 blocks away; plenty of street parking and parking garages
Phone: (415) 512–1281
Hours: 10:00 A.M.–6:00 P.M., Monday–Friday; 9:30 A.M.–6:00 P.M., Saturday; noon–5:00 P.M., Sunday
Additional Savings: January and August sales on all earrings. Also, special purchases are always available on earrings.
Credit Cards: American Express, MasterCard, Visa
Personal Checks: Yes
Handicapped Accessible: Yes
Food: Chevy's 1 block away
Bus Tours: Yes
Notes or Attractions: Near San Francisco Center Shopping Mall, Union Square, Moscone Convention Center

Isda & Co.
324 Ritch Street

Directions: South of Market area
Phone: (415) 512–1610
Hours: 10:00 A.M.–5:30 P.M., Monday–Saturday
Credit Cards: MasterCard, Visa
Personal Checks: Yes
Handicapped Accessible: Yes
Food: In the vicinity
Bus Tours: No

Jeanne-Marcdowns
508 Third Street

Directions: South of Market area
Phone: (415) 243–4396
Hours: 11:00 A.M.–5:00 P.M., Monday–Saturday
Credit Cards: MasterCard, Visa
Personal Checks: Yes (San Francisco area only)
Handicapped Accessible: Yes
Food: Nearby
Bus Tours: No

Lady N' I
588 Third Street

Directions: South of Union Square; 2 blocks from Moscone Center; located at the corner of Brannan and Third Street
Phone: (415) 243–8922
Hours: 10:00 A.M.–5:00 P.M., Monday–Saturday
Credit Cards: American Express, MasterCard, Visa
Personal Checks: Yes
Handicapped Accessible: No
Food: Next door
Bus Tours: Yes
Notes or Attractions: More than 200 other outlets in the area; minutes to Pier 39

Lili Ann Outlet
2701 Sixteenth Street

Directions: South of Market area
Phone: (415) 863–2720
Hours: Call for hours.
Credit Cards: MasterCard, Visa
Personal Checks: Yes, with proper identification
Handicapped Accessible: Yes
Food: Nearby

Linen Factory Outlet
475 Ninth Street

Directions: Between Bryant and Harrison in San Francisco's South of Market Street area
Phone: (415) 431–4543
Hours: Noon–4:00 P.M., Monday–Friday; 10:00 A.M.–4:00 P.M., Saturday
Additional Savings: Some items are always on "special," and "very special" sales are available to those on the mailing list.
Credit Cards: Diners Club, MasterCard, Visa
Personal Checks: Yes, with identification
Handicapped Accessible: Yes
Food: Nice restaurants within walking distance
Bus Tours: Yes
Notes or Attractions: Other factory outlets nearby

Malson's Ragsmatazz
622 Clement Street

Directions: Call ahead.
Phone: (415) 221–2854
Hours: 10:00 A.M.–6:00 P.M., Monday–Saturday
Credit Cards: MasterCard, Visa
Personal Checks: Yes, with driver's license (no post-office-box addresses)
Handicapped Accessible: Yes
Food: Nearby
Bus Tours: Yes

Malson's Ragsmatazz
493 Third Street

Directions: South of Market area
Phone: (415) 495–5037
Hours: 10:00 A.M.–6:00 P.M., Monday–Saturday
Credit Cards: MasterCard, Visa
Personal Checks: Yes, with driver's license (no post-office-box addresses)
Handicapped Accessible: Yes
Food: Nearby
Bus Tours: Yes

Mill Valley Cotton Outlet
470 Third Street

Directions: South of Market Street; can be reached from Highway 101 and Bay Bridge
Phone: (415) 495–2001
Hours: 9:00 A.M.–5:00 P.M., Wednesday–Saturday
Additional Savings: Five-dollar bargain area for damaged merchandise
Credit Cards: MasterCard, Visa
Personal Checks: Yes
Handicapped Accessible: No
Food: A great sushi restaurant across the street, a cafe next door, a Mexican restaurant 2 blocks west, and more
Bus Tours: Yes, under the overpass
Notes or Attractions: Many other outlets nearby

Multiple Choices
899 Howard Street

Directions: South of Market area
Phone: (415) 495–2628
Hours: 9:30 A.M.–6:30 P.M., Monday–Saturday; noon–5:00 P.M., Sunday
Credit Cards: MasterCard, Visa
Personal Checks: Yes
Handicapped Accessible: Yes

Food: Within walking distance
Bus Tours: Yes

New West
426 Brannan Street

Directions: South of Market Street
Phone: (415) 882–4929
Hours: Noon–6:00 P.M., Monday–Saturday; noon–5:00 P.M., Sunday
Credit Cards: American Express, MasterCard, Visa
Personal Checks: Yes, with proper identification
Handicapped Accessible: Yes
Food: Nearby
Bus Tours: No

New York Cosmetics & Fragrances
674 Eighth Street

Directions: South of Market area
Phone: (415) 621–4445
Hours: 10:00 A.M.–5:00 P.M., Monday–Friday; call for Saturday hours.
Credit Cards: Discover, MasterCard, Visa
Personal Checks: Yes
Handicapped Accessible: Yes
Food: Nearby
Notes or Attractions: Also order by mail, telephone, or fax.

New York Cosmetics & Fragrances
318 Brannan Street

Directions: South of Market area
Phone: (415) 543–3880
Hours: 11:00 A.M.–5:30 P.M., Monday–Friday; 10:00 A.M.–5:00 P.M., Saturday; call for Sunday hours.
Credit Cards: Discover, MasterCard, Visa
Personal Checks: Yes

Handicapped Accessible: Yes
Food: Nearby
Notes or Attractions: Also order by mail, telephone, or fax.

Next Express
1315 Howard Street

Directions: South of Market Street between Ninth Street and Tenth Street
Phone: (415) 255–1311
Hours: 10:00 A.M.–6:00 P.M., Monday–Saturday; noon–6:00 P.M., Sunday
Additional Savings: Sales on major summer holidays
Credit Cards: MasterCard, Visa
Personal Checks: Yes, with driver's license or identification
Handicapped Accessible: Yes
Food: Within 1 block
Bus Tours: Yes
Notes or Attractions: Near other outlets and subway

North Face Factory Outlet
1325 Howard Street

Directions: South of Market Street at Ninth Street and Howard Street
Phone: (415) 626–6444
Hours: 10:00 A.M.–8:00 P.M., Monday–Thursday; 10:00 A.M.–6:00 P.M., Friday–Saturday; 11:00 A.M.–5:00 P.M., Sunday
Additional Savings: Monthly specials as well as three large sales events a year
Credit Cards: American Express, Discover, MasterCard, Visa
Personal Checks: Yes
Handicapped Accessible: Yes
Food: Available 1-3 blocks away
Bus Tours: No

Outlet for Contemporary Career Clothing
2565 Third Street

Directions: South of Market area
Phone: (415) 285–7177
Hours: Call for hours.
Credit Cards: No
Personal Checks: Yes
Handicapped Accessible: Yes
Food: Nearby
Bus Tours: No

Rainbeau Bodywear
300 Fourth Street

Directions: Coming from 101/280, take Seventh Street exit, veer left onto Seventh Street, go to the right lane, and take a left on Folsom; located on the corner of Folsom and Fourth Street. From the East Bay, take the downtown Fifth Street exit, go to Folsom, and turn right to Fourth Street.
Phone: (415) 777–9786
Hours: 10:00 A.M.–5:30 P.M., Monday–Friday; 10:00 A.M.–5:00 P.M., Saturday
Additional Savings: Join the mailing list and receive flyers on upcoming sales.
Credit Cards: American Express, MasterCard, Visa
Personal Checks: Yes, with photograph identification (driver's license or California identification)
Handicapped Accessible: Yes
Food: Chevy's and Max's Diner 1 block away
Bus Tours: No
Notes or Attractions: Ansel Adams Gallery nearby

Ritch Street Outlet
330 Ritch Street

Directions: Located between Townsend and Brannan, take first alley off Third Street toward Fourth Street. Follow sandwich-board signs to

middle of block on Ritch Street. Outlet is located on side of building. Look for red-and-white banner.
Phone: (415) 546–1908
Hours: 11:00 A.M.–5:00 P.M., Monday–Friday; 10:00 A.M.–5:00 P.M., Saturday
Additional Savings: January and periodic storewide sales
Credit Cards: MasterCard, Visa
Personal Checks: Yes
Handicapped Accessible: Yes
Food: Some facilities in the same building and more a half-block away
Bus Tours: Yes
Notes or Attractions: Near many other outlets

Rock Express
350 Spear Street

Directions: South of Market area
Phone: (415) 597–9799
Hours: Noon–6:00 P.M., Wednesday–Friday; 10:00 A.M.–4:00 P.M., Saturday
Credit Cards: American Express, MasterCard, Visa
Personal Checks: Yes
Handicapped Accessible: Yes
Food: Nearby

Rug Resource
524 Third Street

Directions: South of Market area
Phone: (415) 543–7600
Hours: 9:00 A.M.–6:00 P.M., Monday–Saturday; noon–5:00 P.M., Sunday
Credit Cards: American Express, MasterCard, Visa
Personal Checks: Yes
Handicapped Accessible: Yes
Food: In the area
Bus Tours: Yes
Notes or Attractions: Free parking adjacent to the store

Salina Fashion
899 Howard Street

Directions: South of Market area
Phone: (415) 777-3089
Hours: 10:00 A.M.–6:00 P.M., Monday–Saturday; noon–5:00 P.M., Sunday
Credit Cards: MasterCard, Visa
Personal Checks: Yes
Handicapped Accessible: Yes
Food: Within walking distance
Bus Tours: Yes

Sandra Ingrish Outlet
1000 Brannan Street (Third Floor)

Directions: South of Market Street area; cross streets are Ninth and Brannan
Phone: (415) 864-5545
Hours: 10:00 A.M.–4:00 P.M., Saturday only
Credit Cards: No
Personal Checks: Yes
Handicapped Accessible: Yes
Food: Restaurants 2 blocks away
Bus Tours: Yes

San Francisco City Lights Outlet
333 Ninth Street

Directions: From 101 North, take Ninth Street exit up 2 blocks. From Bay Bridge, take Ninth Street exit, turn right on Ninth Street, and go 1 block. From Golden Gate, take Lombard to Van Ness and take Van Ness south to Division; turn left and go to Bryant; turn left and go to Ninth Street; make a left on Ninth Street and go up 2 blocks.
Phone: (415) 861-6063
Hours: 10:00 A.M.–6:00 P.M., Monday–Saturday
Additional Savings: Blowout sale twice a year
Credit Cards: MasterCard, Visa; ATM Debit

Personal Checks: Yes
Handicapped Accessible: No
Food: Many restaurants within walking distance
Bus Tours: No
Notes or Attractions: Close to freeway and Civic Center

Shoe Pavilion
899 Howard Street

Directions: South of Market area
Phone: (415) 974–1821
Hours: 9:30 A.M.–8:00 P.M., Monday–Saturday; 11:00 A.M.–6:00 P.M., Sunday
Credit Cards: American Express, Discover, MasterCard, Visa
Personal Checks: Yes, with driver's license and major credit card
Handicapped Accessible: Yes
Food: Within walking distance
Bus Tours: Yes

Simply Cotton
610 Third Street

Directions: South of Market area
Phone: (415) 543–2058
Hours: 10:00 A.M.–5:00 P.M., Monday–Friday
Credit Cards: MasterCard, Visa
Personal Checks: Yes, with driver's license
Handicapped Accessible: Yes
Food: Nearby

660 Center
660 Third Street

Directions: Located on Third Street between Brannan and Townsend Street in the South of Market area
Phone: (415) 227–0464

Hours: 10:00 A.M.–5:30 P.M., Monday–Saturday; noon–5:00 P.M., Sunday
Outlets:
BC Jewelry and Gifts
Carole's Shoe Heaven
Cotton Candy
Designer Man-Woman
Dress Market
Her Lingerie
Jamis Wear
Kidswear Center
Madelle's
Magnolia
Newport Outlet
Outerwear Company
Saratoga Sport Outlet
SF Fashion Outlet
Sister Sister
Ultimate Boutique
Credit Cards: Most major cards
Personal Checks: Most stores accept checks with proper identification.
Handicapped Accessible: Yes
Food: Center Court Cafe located in mall; also twenty restaurants within
1-block area
Bus Tours: Yes
Notes or Attractions: Free parking

Spare Changes
695 Third Street

Directions: Call ahead.
Phone: (415) 342–3248
Hours: 9:30 A.M.–5:30 P.M., Monday–Saturday; 11:00 A.M.–4:00 P.M., Sunday
Additional Savings: Twice-yearly clearance with deep discounts; always
a clearance rack with great deals
Credit Cards: MasterCard, Visa
Personal Checks: Yes, with identification

Handicapped Accessible: Yes
Food: Within 1 block
Notes or Attractions: Near many other outlets in South of Market area; convenient layaway program

Sparkle Plenty Too
425 Brannan Street

Directions: Located between Third Street and Fourth Street
Phone: (415) 243–9551
Hours: 10:00 A.M.–5:00 P.M., Monday–Saturday
Additional Savings: Two special sales a year
Credit Cards: MasterCard, Visa
Personal Checks: Yes
Handicapped Accessible: No
Food: Within 2 blocks
Bus Tours: Yes
Notes or Attractions: Close to many other outlets and great restaurants

Stubbies Outlet
899 Howard Street

Directions: South of Market area
Phone: (415) 495–2628
Hours: 9:30 A.M.–8:00 P.M., Monday–Saturday; 11:00 A.M.–6:00 P.M., Sunday
Credit Cards: MasterCard, Visa
Personal Checks: Yes
Handicapped Accessible: Yes
Food: Within walking distance
Bus Tours: Yes

Tight End
434 Ninth Street

Directions: South of Market area between Bryant and Harrison

Phone: (415) 255–8881
Hours: 10:00 A.M.–4:00 P.M., Monday–Saturday
Credit Cards: No
Personal Checks: Yes
Handicapped Accessible: Yes
Food: In the vicinity
Bus Tours: No

T.J.'s Factory Store
592 Third Street

Directions: South of Market area
Phone: (415) 974–1760
Hours: 10:00 A.M.–5:00 P.M., Monday–Saturday
Credit Cards: No
Personal Checks: Yes
Handicapped Accessible: Yes
Food: Nearby
Bus Tours: No

Townsend Clearance Center
242 Townsend Street

Directions: South of Market area
Phone: (415) 777–4578
Hours: 10:00 A.M.–5:00 P.M., Monday–Saturday
Credit Cards: Major cards accepted
Personal Checks: Yes
Handicapped Accessible: Yes
Food: Nearby
Bus Tours: No

Toy Liquidators
899 Howard Street

Directions: Call ahead.
Phone: (415) 243–8518

Hours: 9:30 A.M.–7:00 P.M., Monday–Saturday; 11:00 A.M.–5:00 P.M., Sunday
Credit Cards: Discover, MasterCard, Visa
Personal Checks: Yes
Handicapped Accessible: Yes
Food: Within 1 block
Bus Tours: Yes

UP Fashion Clearance Center
420 Bryant Street

Directions: From Bay Bridge, take Freemont Street exit, turn left on Harrison Street, and go to Fourth Street; turn left on Fourth Street and then right on Bryant Street. From San Jose, take Highway 101 North to Highway 880 Bay Bridge and exit at Fourth Street; follow exit to the left onto Bryant Street.
Phone: (415) 957–1676
Hours: 10:00 A.M.–4:00 P.M., Monday–Saturday
Additional Savings: Seasonal sales for preferred-customer mailing list
Credit Cards: MasterCard, Visa
Personal Checks: Yes, with two forms of identification
Handicapped Accessible: Yes
Food: Available 1-2 blocks away
Bus Tours: Yes
Notes or Attractions: Near other factory outlets

Van Heusen
601 Mission Street

Directions: Call ahead.
Phone: (415) 243–0750
Hours: 8:00 A.M.–6:00 P.M., Monday–Thursday; 8:00 A.M.–8:00 P.M., Friday; 9:00 A.M.–6:00 P.M., Saturday; 11:00 A.M.–5:00 P.M., Sunday
Credit Cards: Discover, MasterCard, Visa
Personal Checks: Yes
Handicapped Accessible: Yes
Food: Nearby
Bus Tours: No

San Jose

Burlington Coat Factory
1600 Saratoga Avenue

Directions: Call ahead.
Phone: (408) 378–2628
Hours: 10:00 A.M.–9:30 P.M., Monday–Friday; 10:00 A.M.–7:00 P.M., Saturday; 10:00 A.M.–6:00 P.M., Sunday
Additional Savings: Warehouse Coat Sale last two weeks of January
Credit Cards: American Express, Discover, MasterCard, Visa
Personal Checks: Yes
Handicapped Accessible: Yes
Food: Fresh Choice Salad Bar, Frogg Lane Bar & Grill, Asadas Mexican Cafe, Strings Pasta Place, and Bon Croissant Bakery & Sandwich Shop all nearby
Bus Tours: Yes
Notes or Attractions: Great American Amusement Park (4 miles), Winchester Mystery House (2 miles), Children's Discovery Museum (4 miles), Old Town Los Gatos (2 miles), Egyptian Museum and Planetarium (5 miles), Paul Masson Mountain Winery and Theater (10 miles), Santa Cruz Beach and Boardwalk (25 miles)

Six Star Factory Outlet
Hacienda Gardens Shopping Center
3065 Meridian Avenue

Directions: Call ahead.
Phone: (408) 265–0221
Hours: 9:30 A.M.–9:00 P.M., Monday–Friday; 9:30 A.M.–6:00 P.M., Saturday; 10:30 A.M.–6:00 P.M., Sunday
Credit Cards: MasterCard, Visa
Personal Checks: Yes
Handicapped Accessible: Yes
Food: Available in the vicinity
Bus Tours: Yes

Six Star Factory Outlet
Mt. Pleasant Shopping Center
3050 Story Road

Directions: Call ahead.
Phone: (408) 729–0144
Hours: 9:30 A.M.–9:00 P.M., Monday–Friday; 9:30 A.M.–6:00 P.M., Saturday; 9:30 A.M.–5:45 P.M., Sunday
Credit Cards: MasterCard, Visa
Personal Checks: Yes
Handicapped Accessible: Yes
Food: Available in the vicinity
Bus Tours: Yes

San Leandro

The Glassware Outlet
1265 Marina Boulevard

Directions: From Highway 880, take Marina Boulevard exit.
Phone: (510) 351–2666
Hours: 10:00 A.M.–9:00 P.M., Monday–Friday; 10:00 A.M.–7:00 P.M., Saturday; 11:00 A.M.–6:00 P.M., Sunday
Credit Cards: MasterCard, Visa
Personal Checks: Yes
Handicapped Accessible: Yes
Food: Available 1 to 3 miles away
Bus Tours: Yes

Marina Square Mall
1221 Marina Boulevard

Directions: Take 880 Freeway to Marina Boulevard East exit.
Phone: (510) 351–5600
Hours: 10:00 A.M.–9:00 P.M., Monday–Friday; 10:00 A.M.–6:00 P.M., Saturday; 11:00 A.M.–6:00 P.M., Sunday

Outlets:
Aca Joe
Activewear Outlet
Athlete's Foot
Audrey Jones
Basics Beauty Supply & Salon
Bizmart
Eddie Bauer
$5 Clothing Store
Gap Outlet
Nordstrom Rack
Party America
Publishers Outlet
Simply Cotton
Talbot's
Credit Cards: Most major cards
Personal Checks: Most stores accept checks with proper identification.
Handicapped Accessible: Yes
Food: Marina Bakery & Cafe, Giovelli's Pizzeria, and TCBY Yogurt in the mall
Bus Tours: Yes
Notes or Attractions: Two minutes from Oakland Airport

San Marcos

Burlington Coat Factory
1617 Catalina Road

Directions: Call ahead.
Phone: (619) 471–5437
Hours: 10:00 A.M.–9:00 P.M., Monday–Friday; 10:00 A.M.–7:00 P.M., Saturday; 11:00 A.M.–6:00 P.M., Sunday
Additional Savings: Warehouse Coat Sale last two weeks of January
Credit Cards: American Express, Discover, MasterCard, Visa
Personal Checks: Yes
Handicapped Accessible: Yes

Food: Charley Brown's, Paolos Pizza, and Skinny Haven nearby
Bus Tours: Yes
Notes or Attractions: Near Disneyland, Queen Mary, and Spruce Goose

San Diego North County Factory Outlet Center
1050 Los Vallecitos Boulevard

Directions: From I–15, go west on Freeway 78 to the San Marcos Boulevard exit; continue west across San Marcos Boulevard on frontage road (Los Vallecitos Boulevard) for 1 mile. From I–5, go east on Freeway 78 to the San Marcos Boulevard exit; turn left on San Marcos Boulevard and then left on Los Vallecitos Boulevard; continue on Los Vallecitos Boulevard for 1 mile.
Phone: (619) 471–1591
Hours: 10:00 A.M.–8:00 P.M., Monday–Saturday; 10:00 A.M.–6:00 P.M., Sunday
Outlets:
Adolfo II
Aileen
Arrow Factory Store
Black & Decker
Bon Worth
Book Warehouse
Bugle Boy
Capezio
Corning/Revere
Designer Kids
Designer Labels For Less – Men
Designer Labels For Less – Women
Famous Brands Housewares
Famous Footwear
Izod
Leather Loft
L'eggs/Hanes/Bali
Paper Factory/Paper Outlet
Perfumania
Socks Galore

Toy Liquidators
Trend Club
Welcome Home
Westport Ltd.
Whims-Sarah Coventry Outlet
Credit Cards: Most major cards
Personal Checks: Most stores accept checks with proper identification.
Handicapped Accessible: Yes
Food: Cafe 78 and La Jolla Cafe & Carts in the mall
Bus Tours: Yes
Notes or Attractions: San Diego area's only enclosed, air-conditioned factory outlet center

San Mateo

Spare Changes
1324 West Hillsdale Boulevard

Directions: Call ahead.
Phone: (415) 573–9113
Hours: 10:00 A.M.–7:00 P.M., Monday–Friday; 10:00 A.M.–6:00 P.M., Saturday; 11:00 A.M.–4:00 P.M., Sunday
Additional Savings: Twice-yearly clearance with deep discounts; always a clearance rack with great deals
Credit Cards: MasterCard, Visa
Personal Checks: Yes, with identification
Handicapped Accessible: Yes
Food: Within 1 block
Bus Tours: No

San Rafael

Ballerini Italian Clothing
3680 Northgate Drive

Directions: From San Francisco, take 101 North; exit Terra Linda (stay in left lane); go to second traffic light and turn left. From Santa Rosa or northern Marin County, take 101 South; exit Terra Linda; at second traffic light, turn left. Located across from Mervyn's parking lot.

Phone: (415) 499–8812

Hours: 10:00 A.M.–8:00 P.M., Monday–Friday; 11:00 A.M.–6:00 P.M., Saturday–Sunday

Credit Cards: American Express, Discover, MasterCard, Visa

Personal Checks: Yes

Handicapped Accessible: No

Food: Within a three-minute walk

Bus Tours: Yes

Notes or Attractions: Sears, Mervyn's, and many other stores are located in this mall.

Santa Ana

Nordstrom Rack
3900 South Bristol

Directions: Call ahead.

Phone: (714) 751–5901

Hours: 9:30 A.M.–9:00 P.M., Monday–Friday; 9:30 A.M.–7:00 P.M., Saturday; 10:00 A.M.–6:00 P.M., Sunday

Additional Savings: Legendary 25- and 50-percent off sales

Credit Cards: American Express, MasterCard, Nordstrom, Visa

Personal Checks: Yes, with two forms of identification

Handicapped Accessible: Yes

Food: Nearby

Bus Tours: Yes, call ahead for information.

Santa Barbara

Firenze
419 State Street

Directions: Take 101 and exit at Garden Street; take to Garden Street to Gutierrez Street and turn left; go to State Street and park in public parking lot on left corner. Store is in the next block.

Phone: (805) 965–5723
Hours: 10:00 A.M.–5:30 P.M., Monday–Saturday; 10:00 A.M.–6:00 P.M., Sunday
Additional Savings: Annual Blowout Sale February–March (30 to 80 percent off factory prices); Preseason Sale August–September (40 to 70 percent off factory prices).
Credit Cards: American Express, MasterCard, Visa
Personal Checks: Yes
Handicapped Accessible: Yes
Food: Within 1 block
Bus Tours: Yes
Notes or Attractions: Santa Barbara is a tourist mecca.

Santa Monica

The Framing Center
2602 Santa Monica Boulevard

Directions: Call ahead.
Phone: (310) 453–1512
Hours: 10:00 A.M.–6:00 P.M., Tuesday–Saturday
Additional Savings: March–April, summer, and Christmas sales
Credit Cards: MasterCard, Visa
Personal Checks: Yes
Handicapped Accessible: Yes
Food: One block away
Bus Tours: Yes
Notes or Attractions: Santa Monica Promenade nearby

San Ysidro

San Diego Factory Outlet Center
4498 Camino de la Plaza

Directions: Southbound: Take I-5 or 805 toward the international border; exit at Camino de la Plaza (sign reads LAST US EXIT) and turn right; go 1 block and look for the center on the right. Northbound: Take I-5 to sign for VIA DE SAN YSIDRO BLVD and turn left; go to stop sign, turn left, and follow the road around until it turns into Camino de la Plaza; look for the center on the left. By trolley: Take trolley to the end of the line, walk north 1 block, and turn left on Camino de la Plaza.

Phone: (619) 690–2999

Hours: 10:00 A.M.–8:00 P.M., Monday–Friday; 10:00 A.M.–7:00 P.M., Saturday; 10:00 A.M.–6:00 P.M., Sunday

Outlets:
Accessorize Fashion Jewelry
Adolfo II
Aileen
Banister Shoes
Bass
Black & Decker
Book Warehouse
Corning/Revere
Designer Brands Accessories
Eddie Bauer
Famous Brands Housewares
Fieldcrest Cannon
Firenze
G&G Nintendo-Sega Outlet
Georgiou Outlet
Gitano
Izod/Gant
Leather Loft
Levi's
Maidenform
Marika
Mikasa
Multiples
Nike
PFC Fragrance & Cosmetics
Polly Flinders
The Ribbon Outlet, Inc.
Star Baby
Toy Liquidators
Van Heusen

Wallet Works
Welcome Home
Credit Cards: Most major cards
Personal Checks: Most stores accept checks with proper identification.
Handicapped Accessible: Yes
Food: Filippi's Family Restaurant located in mall
Bus Tours: Yes
Notes or Attractions: Postal Center in mall

Sausalito

Bali Importers Outlet
595 Bridgeway

Directions: Call ahead.
Phone: (415) 332–3537
Hours: 10:00 A.M.–9:00 P.M., Monday–Sunday
Credit Cards: MasterCard, Visa
Personal Checks: Yes
Handicapped Accessible: Yes
Food: Within walking distance
Bus Tours: Yes

Georgiou Outlet
579 Bridgeway

Directions: On main street in Sausalito (Bridgeway)
Phone: (415) 331–0579
Hours: Call ahead for current hours.
Credit Cards: American Express, Discover, MasterCard, Visa
Personal Checks: Yes
Handicapped Accessible: Yes
Food: Great choices nearby
Bus Tours: Yes
Notes or Attractions: Small-town ambience; shopping/tourist area; great ferry ride from San Francisco

Sherman Oaks

L.A. Framing Mart
4362 Woodman Avenue

Directions: Call ahead.
Phone: (818) 907–9229
Hours: 10:00 A.M.–6:00 P.M., Monday–Saturday
Additional Savings: March–April, summer, and Christmas sales
Credit Cards: MasterCard, Visa
Personal Checks: Yes
Handicapped Accessible: Yes
Food: One block away
Bus Tours: Yes

Solvang

Welcome Home
485 Alisal Road

Directions: Call ahead.
Phone: (505) 686–1554
Hours: 9:00 A.M.–8:00 P.M., Monday–Saturday; 9:00 A.M.–6:00 P.M., Sunday
Credit Cards: American Express, Discover, MasterCard, Visa
Personal Checks: Yes
Handicapped Accessible: Yes
Food: Nearby
Bus Tours: Yes

South Lake Tahoe

Great Outdoor Clothing Co.
2050 Lake Tahoe Boulevard

Directions: Call ahead.
Phone: (916) 541–0664

Hours: 10:00 A.M.–7:00 P.M., Monday–Sunday
Credit Cards: Discover, MasterCard, Visa
Personal Checks: Yes
Handicapped Accessible: Yes
Food: In the area
Bus Tours: Yes

Home Again
2030 Lake Tahoe Boulevard

Directions: Call ahead.
Phone: (916) 541–6914
Hours: 9:00 A.M.–7:00 P.M., Monday–Sunday
Credit Cards: American Express, Discover, MasterCard, Visa
Personal Checks: Yes
Handicapped Accessible: Yes
Food: Nearby
Bus Tours: Yes

Prestige Fragrance & Cosmetics
2501 Lake Tahoe Boulevard #B

Directions: From casinos, drive south on Lake Tahoe Boulevard approximately 4 to 5 miles; located just past Sierra Boulevard, on the right. From Placerville or Emerald Bay, drive north on Lake Tahoe Boulevard approximately ¼ mile; located on the left.
Phone: (916) 542–2436
Hours: Summer: 9:30 A.M.–6:30 P.M., Monday–Saturday; 10:00 A.M.–5:00 P.M., Sunday. Winter: 10:00 A.M.–6:00 P.M., Monday–Saturday; 10:00 A.M.–5:00 P.M., Sunday.
Additional Savings: Every month ten different items are marked down further than regular low price.
Credit Cards: American Express, MasterCard, Visa
Personal Checks: Yes
Handicapped Accessible: Yes
Food: Carrows 1 block away; Mexican Cafe across the street; several fast-food and conventional restaurants within a 3-mile range

Bus Tours: Yes
Notes or Attractions: Minigolf, arcade, and carnival for children; other factory stores ¼ mile away

Van Heusen
2032 Lake Tahoe Boulevard

Directions: Located at the intersection of Highway 50 and Emerald Bay Road (Highway 89) in South Lake Tahoe
Phone: (916) 541–8314
Hours: 9:00 A.M.–7:00 P.M., Monday–Sunday
Additional Savings: Summer clearance
Credit Cards: Discover, MasterCard, Visa
Personal Checks: Yes
Handicapped Accessible: Yes
Food: Quite a few restaurants nearby
Bus Tours: Yes
Notes or Attractions: Gambling in Lake Tahoe

Torrance

Krause's Sofa Factory
20901 Hawthorne Boulevard

Directions: Call ahead.
Phone: (310) 542–4511
Hours: 10:00 A.M.–9:00 P.M., Monday–Friday; 10:00 A.M.–6:00 P.M., Saturday–Sunday
Additional Savings: Semiannual sale (two per year)
Credit Cards: Discover, MasterCard, Visa
Personal Checks: Yes
Handicapped Accessible: Yes
Food: In the vicinity
Bus Tours: No

Truckee

Bass
12047 Donner Pass Road, Suite A-2

Directions: Take Donner Pass Road exit off I–80.
Phone: (916) 587–9290
Hours: 9:30 A.M.–6:00 P.M., Monday–Sunday
Additional Savings: Promotions are run on a biweekly basis; also "Back-to-School" sales, etc.
Credit Cards: Discover, MasterCard, Visa
Personal Checks: Yes
Handicapped Accessible: Yes
Food: Within walking distance; also, downtown Truckee (2 miles away) has a great variety of restaurants.
Bus Tours: Yes
Notes or Attractions: Close to Old Truckee and Donner Lake

Great Outdoor Clothing Co.
11310 Donner Pass Road, #5 and #6

Directions: Call ahead.
Phone: (916) 582–1990
Hours: 10:00 A.M.–8:00 P.M., Monday–Saturday; 10:00 A.M.–6:00 P.M., Sunday
Credit Cards: Discover, MasterCard, Visa
Personal Checks: Yes
Handicapped Accessible: Yes
Food: In the area
Bus Tours: Yes

Home Again
12047 Donner Pass Road

Directions: Call ahead.
Phone: (916) 582–0839
Hours: 9:00 A.M.–6:00 P.M., Monday–Sunday

Credit Cards: American Express, Discover, MasterCard, Visa
Personal Checks: Yes
Handicapped Accessible: Yes
Food: Nearby
Bus Tours: Yes

Swank
12047 Donner Pass Road, #B-7

Directions: From eastbound I–80, take the Donner Lake exit and turn left over the freeway. From westbound I–80, take the same exit and turn right.
Phone: (916) 582–0558
Hours: 9:30 A.M.–6:00 P.M., Monday–Sunday
Credit Cards: MasterCard, Visa
Personal Checks: Yes
Handicapped Accessible: Yes
Food: Mt. Grill is next door.
Bus Tours: Yes
Notes or Attractions: Near Donner State Park, Squaw Valley, and Donner Lake

Union City

Six Star Factory Outlet
El Mercado Plaza
1779 DeCoto Road

Directions: Call ahead.
Phone: (510) 429–1831
Hours: 10:00 A.M.–8:00 P.M., Monday–Friday; 10:00 A.M.–6:00 P.M., Saturday–Sunday
Credit Cards: MasterCard, Visa
Personal Checks: Yes
Handicapped Accessible: Yes
Food: Available in the vicinity
Bus Tours: Yes

Vacaville

Factory Stores at Nut Tree
321–2 Nut Tree Road

Directions: Call ahead.
Phone: (707) 447–5755
Hours: 10:00 A.M.–8:00 P.M., Monday–Saturday; 10:00 A.M.–6:00 P.M., Sunday
Outlets:
Aca Joe
Accessorize Fashion Jewelry
Adolfo II
Aileen
American Tourister
Banister Shoes
Barbizon Lingerie
Bass
Bon Worth
Book Warehouse
Boot Factory/Genesco
Brass Factory Outlet Store
Bugle Boy
Cami'z
Cape Isle Knitters
Capezio
Converse
Corning/Revere
Country Clutter
Crisa
Crystal Works
CYA
Czavra
Designer Brands Accessories
Designer Man-Woman
Diamonds Direct
Etienne Aigner
Evan-Picone

Famous Brands Housewares
Famous Footwear
Firenze
Full Size Fashions
Geoffrey Beene
Gitano
Great Outdoor Clothing Co.
Hanes Activewear
harvé benard
Home Again
IYA
Johnston & Murphy
Jordache
Kid's Zone
Kitchen Collection
Larenda Wallets Etc.
Leather Loft
L'eggs/Hanes/Bali
Leslie Fay
Levi's
Lise J
Maidenform
Naturalizer
New York Express
9 West
Omid International Rugs
Oneida
Paper Factory/Paper Outlet
Perfumania
PFC Fragrance & Cosmetics
Polly Flinders
Reebok
The Ribbon Outlet, Inc.
Royal Doulton
Ruff Hewn
Sam & Libby
Sbicca Shoes
Sergio Tacchini

Shoe Outlet
Silver & More
Simply Cotton
Socks Galore
Sportif USA
Star Baby
The Sweatshirt Company
Toy Liquidators
Trend Club
United Colors of Benetton
Van Heusen
Wemco
West Point Pepperell
Westport Ltd.
Westport Woman
Wicker Factory
Credit Cards: Most major cards
Personal Checks: Most stores accept checks with proper identification.
Handicapped Accessible: Yes
Food: Food pavilion and Louie's Place Deli located in the mall complex
Bus Tours: Yes
Notes or Attractions: Shopper's Shuttle runs daily from 11:00 A.M. to 6:00 P.M.

Van Nuys

Krause's Sofa Factory
15600 Roscoe Boulevard

Directions: Call ahead.
Phone: (818) 994–6046
Hours: 10:00 A.M.–9:00 P.M., Monday–Friday; 10:00 A.M.–6:00 P.M., Saturday–Sunday
Additional Savings: Semiannual sale (two per year)
Credit Cards: Discover, MasterCard, Visa
Personal Checks: Yes

Handicapped Accessible: Yes
Food: In the vicinity
Bus Tours: No

Vista

Upholstery Fabric Outlet (UFO)
1120 North Melrose Drive

Directions: Take Highway 78 (which runs between I–5 and I–15) and exit Melrose Drive North. Go about 1 mile; outlet will be on the right.
Phone: (619) 941–2345
Hours: 9:00 A.M.–5:30 P.M., Monday–Saturday
Credit Cards: MasterCard, Visa
Personal Checks: Yes
Handicapped Accessible: Yes
Food: A number of restaurants within five to ten minutes drive
Bus Tours: Yes
Notes or Attractions: This outlet is located an hour to an hour and a half south of Los Angeles.

West Hills

JC Penney Catalog Outlet Store
6651 Fallbrook Avenue

Directions: Take the 101 Freeway to Fallbrook exit. Store is located between Victory and Vanowen.
Phone: (818) 883–3660
Hours: 9:30 A.M.–9:00 P.M., Monday–Friday; 9:30 A.M.–7:00 P.M., Saturday; 10:00 A.M.–6:00 P.M., Sunday
Credit Cards: American Express, JC Penney, MasterCard, Visa
Personal Checks: Yes, with California identification
Handicapped Accessible: Yes
Food: Fallbrook Mall has a large food court, and there are at least half a

dozen restaurants within walking distance.
Bus Tours: Yes
Notes or Attractions: Close to General Cinema

Woodland

Six Star Factory Outlet
West Court Plaza Shopping Center
52 West Court Street

Directions: Call ahead.
Phone: (916) 666–9035
Hours: 9:30 A.M.–8:00 P.M., Monday–Friday; 9:30 A.M.–7:00 P.M., Saturday; 10:00 A.M.–6:00 P.M., Sunday
Credit Cards: MasterCard, Visa
Personal Checks: Yes
Handicapped Accessible: Yes
Food: Available in the vicinity
Bus Tours: Yes

Woodland Hills

Nordstrom Rack
21490 Victory Boulevard

Directions: Call ahead.
Phone: (818) 884–6771
Hours: 10:00 A.M.–9:00 P.M., Monday–Friday; 10:00 A.M.–7:00 P.M., Saturday; 11:00 A.M.–6:00 P.M., Sunday
Additional Savings: Legendary 25-percent and 50-percent off sales
Credit Cards: American Express, MasterCard, Nordstrom, Visa
Personal Checks: Yes, with two forms of identification
Handicapped Accessible: Yes
Food: Nearby
Bus Tours: Yes; call ahead for information.

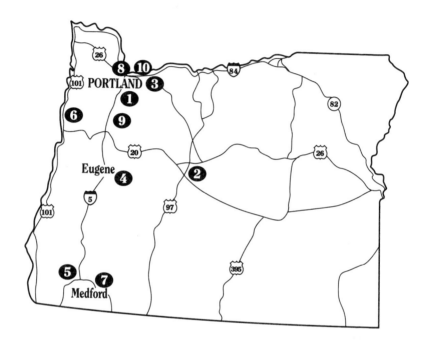

Oregon

Numbers to the left of entries in this legend correspond to the numbers on the accompanying map. The number to the right of each city's or town's name is the page number on which that municipality's outlets first appear.

Beaverton

Burlington Coat Factory
8775 S.W. Cascade Avenue

Directions: Call ahead.
Phone: (503) 646–9900
Hours: 10:00 A.M.–9:30 P.M., Monday–Saturday; 10:00 A.M.–6:00 P.M., Sunday
Additional Savings: Warehouse Coat Sale last two weeks of January
Credit Cards: American Express, Discover, MasterCard, Visa
Personal Checks: Yes
Handicapped Accessible: Yes
Food: Zio Chen, Shirley, and Benihana of Tokyo all nearby
Bus Tours: Yes
Notes or Attractions: Located close to Washington Square and Malibu Grand Prix

Bend

Welcome Home
61318 South Highway 97

Directions: Call ahead.
Phone: (503) 389–7050
Hours: Call ahead for hours.
Credit Cards: American Express, Discover, MasterCard, Visa
Personal Checks: Yes
Handicapped Accessible: Yes
Food: Nearby
Bus Tours: Yes

Clackamas

Nordstrom Rack
8930 S.E. Sunnyside Road

Directions: Located south and east of Portland; take Highway 205 to Sunnyside Road exit.
Phone: (503) 654–5415
Hours: 10:00 A.M.–9:00 P.M., Monday–Friday; 10:00 A.M.–7:00 P.M., Saturday; 11:00 A.M.–7:00 P.M., Sunday
Additional Savings: Legendary 25-percent and 50-percent off sales
Credit Cards: American Express, MasterCard, Nordstrom, Visa
Personal Checks: Yes, with two forms of identification
Handicapped Accessible: Yes
Food: Within 1 block
Bus Tours: Yes
Notes or Attractions: Close to Portland Airport; Clackamas Town Center Mall across the street

Eugene

Champion Factory Outlet
1530 Coburg Road

Directions: Call ahead.
Phone: (503) 343–1054
Hours: 9:30 A.M.–9:00 P.M., Monday–Saturday; noon–6:00 P.M., Sunday
Credit Cards: Discover, MasterCard, Visa
Personal Checks: Yes, with driver's license
Handicapped Accessible: Yes
Food: In the area
Bus Tours: Yes

Great Outdoor Clothing Co.
198 West Broadway

Directions: Call ahead.
Phone: (503) 342–6973
Hours: 10:00 A.M.–6:00 P.M., Monday–Friday; 10:00 A.M.–5:30 P.M., Saturday; noon–5:00 P.M., Sunday
Credit Cards: Discover, MasterCard, Visa
Personal Checks: Yes
Handicapped Accessible: Yes
Food: In the area
Bus Tours: Yes

Grants Pass

Champion Factory Outlet
401 Southeast Sixth Street

Directions: Call ahead.
Phone: (503) 479–6414
Hours: 9:30 A.M.–6:00 P.M., Monday–Saturday; noon–5:00 P.M., Sunday
Credit Cards: Discover, MasterCard, Visa
Personal Checks: Yes, with driver's license
Handicapped Accessible: Yes
Food: In the area
Bus Tours: Yes

Lincoln City

Factory Stores at Lincoln City
Highway 101

Directions: On Highway 101 north of Highway 20
Phone: (503) 996–5000
Hours: 9:30 A.M.–8:00 P.M., Monday–Saturday; 9:30 A.M.–6:00 P.M., Sunday
Outlets:

Adolfo II
Aileen
American Tourister
Banister Shoes
Bass
Book Warehouse
Cape Isle Knitters
Capezio
Carter's Childrenswear
Converse
Corning/Revere
Duffel
Eddie Bauer
Full Size Fashions
Gitano
Hanes Activewear
Hang Ten
Izod
John Henry & Friends
Kitchen Collection
L'ccessory
Leather Loft
L'eggs/Hanes/Bali
London Fog
Maidenform
McKenzie Outfitters
Mikasa
Old Mill
Oneida
OshKosh B'Gosh
Paper Factory/Paper Outlet
Perfumania
Pfaltzgraff
Polly Flinders
The Ribbon Outlet, Inc.
Royal Doulton
Sierra Shirts
totes/Sunglass World

Toy Liquidators
Van Heusen
Wallet Works
Welcome Home
Wemco
Westport Ltd.
Credit Cards: Most major cards accepted
Personal Checks: Most stores accept checks with proper identification
Handicapped Accessible: Yes
Food: Chateau Benoit, Snack City, and Sweet Delights located in the mall
Bus Tours: Yes
Notes or Attractions: Near Devil's Lake, Cascade Head, whale watching, art galleries, antiques shops, and serene hiking trails

Medford

London Fog
505 Medford Center

Directions: Call ahead.
Phone: (503) 773–4939
Hours: 10:00 A.M.–6:00 P.M., Monday–Saturday; 11:00 A.M.–5:00 P.M., Sunday
Credit Cards: MasterCard, Visa
Personal Checks: Yes, with two forms of identification
Handicapped Accessible: No
Food: Nearby
Bus Tours: No

Portland

Dehen Knitting Co.
404 N.W. Tenth Avenue

Directions: Located 4 blocks north of Powell's Book Store at the corner of Northwest Tenth Avenue and Flanders; turn off Burnside Street onto

Northwest Tenth Avenue and go north.
Phone: (503) 796–0725
Hours: 10:00 A.M.–5:00 P.M., Monday–Saturday
Additional Savings: Four or five sales per year, usually in January, May, August ("Back to School"), Thanksgiving, and Christmas
Credit Cards: Discover, MasterCard, Visa
Personal Checks: Yes, with a photograph identification and check guarantee, MasterCard, or Visa
Handicapped Accessible: Yes
Food: A few blocks away
Bus Tours: Yes
Notes or Attractions: Art galleries, antique-furniture stores, Hanna Anderson, and specialty design stores all in the vicinity; close to downtown Portland, Willamette River, and Powell's Book Store

Nordstrom Rack
401 S.W. Morrison

Directions: Call ahead.
Phone: (503) 299–1815
Hours: 9:30 A.M.–8:00 P.M., Monday–Friday; 9:30 A.M.–7:00 P.M., Saturday; 11:00 A.M.–6:00 P.M., Sunday
Additional Savings: Legendary 25-percent and 50-percent off sales
Credit Cards: American Express, MasterCard, Nordstrom, Visa
Personal Checks: Yes, with two forms of identification
Handicapped Accessible: Yes
Food: Nearby
Bus Tours: Yes

Sears Outlet
10542 S.E. Washington Street

Directions: Call ahead.
Phone: (503) 257–6144
Hours: 10:00 A.M.–9:00 P.M., Monday–Friday; 10:00 A.M.–6:00 P.M., Saturday–Sunday
Credit Cards: Discover, Sears

Personal Checks: Yes
Handicapped Accessible: Yes
Food: In the vicinity
Bus Tours: Yes

Salem

Champion Factory Outlet
2385 Lancaster Road

Directions: Call ahead.
Phone: (503) 370–9237
Hours: 9:30 A.M.–8:00 P.M., Monday–Friday; 9:30 A.M.–6:00 P.M., Saturday; noon–5:00 P.M., Sunday
Credit Cards: Discover, MasterCard, Visa
Personal Checks: Yes, with driver's license
Handicapped Accessible: Yes
Food: In the area
Bus Tours: Yes

Troutdale

Columbia Gorge Factory Stores
450 N.W. 257th Avenue

Directions: Traveling eastbound on I–84, take exit 17 (fifteen minutes east of downtown Portland). Traveling westbound on I–84, take exit 17 (ten minutes west of Multnomah Falls).
Phone: (503) 669–8060
Hours: January 1–March 15: 10:00 A.M.–6:00 P.M., Monday–Sunday. March 15–December 31: 10:00 A.M.–8:00 P.M., Monday–Saturday; 10:00 A.M.–6:00 P.M., Sunday.
Outlets:
American Tourister
Banister Shoes
Bass
Book Warehouse

Brindar
Brown Shoe Company Outlet
Cape Isle Knitters
CYA
Designer Brands Accessories
Famous Brands Housewares
Famous Footwear
Gitano
Great Outdoor Clothing Co.
Hanes Activewear
Hang Ten
Harry & David
Hathaway
Izod
Jordache
Kitchen Collection
Leather Loft
L'eggs/Hanes/Bali
Maidenform
Norm Thompson
Olga/Warner
Paper Factory/Paper Outlet
Prestige Fragrance & Cosmetics
The Ribbon Outlet, Inc.
Socks Galore
Star Baby
Toy Liquidators
Van Heusen
Welcome Home
Westport Ltd.
Credit Cards: Most major cards accepted
Personal Checks: Most stores accept checks with proper identification
Handicapped Accessible: Yes
Food: Sandwich shop located in the mall
Bus Tours: Yes
Notes or Attractions: Adjacent to the scenic Columbia River Gorge

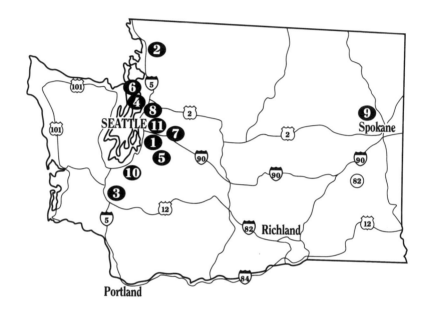

Washington

Numbers to the left of entries in this legend correspond to the numbers on the accompanying map. The number to the right of each city's or town's name is the page number on which that municipality's outlets first appear.

Burien

Sears Outlet
500 Southwest Fifteenth Street

Directions: From I–5, either direction, take Burien exit and follow 518 to First Avenue. Continue straight through light until 4 Southwest. Turn left; go 1 block. Outlet is on the right side of the street next to Payless.
Phone: (206) 241–7000
Hours: 9:30 A.M.–9:00 P.M., Monday–Friday; 9:30 A.M.–7:00 P.M., Saturday; 10:00 A.M.–6:00 P.M., Sunday
Additional Savings: Different sale every month; Super Saturday, Moonlight Madness, Hawaiian Days, etc.
Credit Cards: Discover, Sears
Personal Checks: Yes
Handicapped Accessible: Yes
Food: Burger King ½ block away; 3 Pigs Bar-B-Que in the vicinity
Bus Tours: Yes
Notes or Attractions: Near Payless, Lover's Package, and Stock Market

Burlington

Pacific Edge Outlet Center
234 Fashion Way

Directions: Located at exits 229 and 230 on I–5, Burlington
Phone: (206) 757–3549
Hours: 10:00 A.M.–9:00 P.M., Monday–Saturday; 10:00 A.M.–6:00 P.M., Sunday
Outlets:
Adolfo II
Aileen
American Tourister
Barbizon Lingerie

Cape Isle Knitters
Chicago Cutlery Etc.
Corning/Revere
Evan-Picone
Fashion Flair/Gant
Gitano
Hanes Activewear
harvé benard
I.B. Diffusion
JH Collectibles
Jindo Fur
Jones New York
Jordache
Kitchen Collection
Leather Loft
Liz Claiborne
Maidenform
Mikasa
Prestige Fragrance & Cosmetics
Publishers Outlet
The Ribbon Outlet, Inc.
Shoe Pavilion
Socks Galore
The Sweatshirt Company
Tanner Factory Store
Toys Unlimited
Van Heusen
Wallet Works
Welcome Home
Credit Cards: Major credit cards accepted
Personal Checks: Most stores accept personal checks with proper identification
Handicapped Accessible: Yes
Food: Trade Winds Cafe in the mall
Bus Tours: Yes; call (800) 969–3767

Centralia

Centerville USA
203 North Tower Street

Directions: Call ahead.
Phone: (206) 736–4800
Hours: 9:30 A.M.–5:30 P.M., Monday–Saturday; noon–5:00 P.M., Sunday
Credit Cards: Discover, MasterCard, Visa
Personal Checks: Yes, with identification
Handicapped Accessible: Yes
Food: In the vicinity
Bus Tours: No

Centralia Factory Outlets
I–5, Exit 82

Directions: Take exit 82 off I–5.
Phone: (206) 736–6406
Hours: 10:00 A.M.–5:00 P.M., Monday–Sunday
Outlets:
Aileen
American Tourister
Banister Shoes
Bass
Cape Isle Knitters
Carter's Childrenswear
Churchill Glove
Corning/Revere
Farberware
Fashion Flair
Fieldcrest Cannon
Gitano
Hanes Activewear
John Henry & Friends
Jordache
Kitchen Collection

Leather Loft
L'eggs/Hanes/Bali
Levi's
London Fog
Mushrooms
Old Mill
Oneida
Prestige Fragrance & Cosmetics
Publishers Outlet
The Ribbon Outlet, Inc.
Socks Galore
Swank
totes Factory Stores
Toy Liquidators
Van Heusen
Welcome Home
Credit Cards: Major credit cards accepted
Personal Checks: Most stores accept personal checks with proper iden-
tification
Handicapped Accessible: Yes
Food: A variety of fast-food facilities and restaurants within walking dis-
tance
Bus Tours: Yes
Notes or Attractions: Near Gateway To Mount Saint Helens, Steam
Train, Lewis County Historical Museum, Rhodi Garden, White Pass Ski
Area, and Borst Home

Edmonds

Burlington Coat Factory
Doces Mall
24111 Highway 99

Directions: Call ahead.
Phone: (206) 776–2221
Hours: 10:00 A.M.–9:30 P.M., Monday–Saturday; 10:00 A.M.–6:00 P.M.,
Sunday
Additional Savings: Warehouse Coat Sale last two weeks of January

Credit Cards: American Express, Discover, MasterCard, Visa
Personal Checks: Yes
Handicapped Accessible: Yes
Food: Zio Chen, Shirley, and Benihana of Tokyo all nearby
Bus Tours: Yes
Notes or Attractions: Near Edmonds waterfront place

Kent

Sears Outlet
26020 104th Avenue S.E.

Directions: Call ahead.
Phone: (206) 854–9300
Hours: 9:30 A.M.–9:00 P.M., Monday–Friday; 9:30 A.M.–7:00 P.M., Saturday; 10:00 A.M.–6:00 P.M., Sunday
Credit Cards: Discover, Sears
Personal Checks: Yes
Handicapped Accessible: Yes
Food: In the vicinity
Bus Tours: Yes

Lynwood

Nordstrom Rack
3115 Alderwood Mall Boulevard

Directions: Call ahead.
Phone: (206) 628–2492
Hours: 9:30 A.M.–9:30 P.M., Monday–Friday; 9:30 A.M.–9:00 P.M., Saturday; 11:00 A.M.–6:00 P.M., Sunday
Additional Savings: Legendary 25-percent and 50-percent off sales
Credit Cards: American Express, MasterCard, Nordstrom, Visa
Personal Checks: Yes, with two forms of identification
Handicapped Accessible: Yes
Food: Nearby
Bus Tours: Yes

North Bend

Great Northwest Factory Stores
461 South Fork Avenue S.W.

Directions: From either east or west on I–90, take exit 31. Mall is located at the exit interchange on the north side of the highway.
Phone: (206) 888–4505
Hours: 10:00 A.M.–8:00 P.M., Monday–Saturday; 10:00 A.M.–6:00 P.M., Sunday
Outlets:
Aileen
American Tourister
Banister Shoes
Bass
Book Warehouse
Cami'z
Cape Isle Knitters
Champion/Hanes
Corning/Revere
Czavra
Duffel
Etienne Aigner
Famous Brands Housewares
Famous Footwear
Farberware
Fast Clothing
Fieldcrest Cannon
Gitano
Great Outdoor Clothing Co.
Hathaway
Jordache
Kitchen Collection
L'ccessory
Leather Loft
L'eggs/Hanes/Bali
Olga/Warner
Omid International Rugs

Perfumania
The Ribbon Outlet, Inc.
Socks Galore
The Sweatshirt Company
Toy Liquidators
Van Heusen
Welcome Home
Westport Ltd.
Westport Woman

Credit Cards: Major credit cards accepted

Personal Checks: Most stores accept personal checks with proper identification.

Handicapped Accessible: Yes

Food: In the mall

Bus Tours: Special discounts for bus tours; call (206) 888–4505

Notes or Attractions: Enjoy the spectacular natural beauty of nearby Snoqualmie Falls and Mount Si

Seattle

Nordstrom Rack

1601 Second Avenue

Directions: Call ahead.

Phone: (206) 448–8522

Hours: 9:30 A.M.–7:00 P.M., Monday–Friday; 9:30 A.M.–8:00 P.M., Saturday; 11:00 A.M.–6:00 P.M., Sunday

Additional Savings: Legendary 25-percent and 50-percent off sales

Credit Cards: American Express, MasterCard, Nordstrom, Visa

Personal Checks: Yes, with two forms of identification

Handicapped Accessible: Yes

Food: Nearby

Bus Tours: Yes

Spokane

Burlington Coat Factory
811 West Main Avenue

Directions: Call ahead.
Phone: (509) 747–2628
Hours: 9:30 A.M.–9:30 P.M., Monday–Friday; 9:30 A.M.–7:00 P.M., Saturday; 11:00 A.M.–6:00 P.M., Sunday
Additional Savings: Warehouse Coat Sale last two weeks of January
Credit Cards: American Express, Discover, MasterCard, Visa
Personal Checks: Yes
Handicapped Accessible: Yes
Food: Nearby restaurants include Dim Sum, Hoyts, Sandwich Gardens, Post Street Bar & Grill, Nikkos II, and Olive Garden.
Bus Tours: Yes
Notes or Attractions: Local attractions include Riverfront Park (site of 1974 World's Fair), Main Pavilion, Antique Carousel, Old City Hall Building, and Spokane River

Tacoma

Burlington Coat Factory
Lakewood Mall
10401–5 Gravelly Lake

Directions: Call ahead.
Phone: (206) 588–3595
Hours: 10:00 A.M.–9:30 P.M., Monday–Saturday; 11:00 A.M.–6:00 P.M., Sunday
Additional Savings: Warehouse Coat Sale last two weeks of January
Credit Cards: American Express, Discover, MasterCard, Visa
Personal Checks: Yes
Handicapped Accessible: Yes
Food: La Palma, Charlie Chan's Lakewood Terrace, Lakewood Bar & Grill, Ram's Sports Club Bar & Grill, and Vantage Breakfast House all nearby

Bus Tours: Yes

Notes or Attractions: Nearby attractions include Steilcom Historic District, Ruston waterfront, Fort Defiance Zoo and Park, Fort Lewis and McCord Air Force Base, Tacoma Dome, and Puyallup Fair (in September)

Carter's Childrenswear
1415 Seventy-second Street E.

Directions: Call ahead.
Phone: (206) 472–9340
Hours: 10:00 A.M.–6:00 P.M., Monday–Saturday; noon–5:00 P.M., Sunday
Credit Cards: Discover, MasterCard, Visa
Personal Checks: Yes, with two forms of identification
Handicapped Accessible: Yes
Food: In the vicinity
Bus Tours: No

Sears Outlet
8720 South Tacoma Way

Directions: Call ahead.
Phone: (206) 584–8160
Hours: 10:00 A.M.–9:00 P.M., Monday–Friday; 10:00 A.M.–7:00 P.M., Saturday; 10:00 A.M.–6:00 P.M., Sunday
Credit Cards: Discover, Sears
Personal Checks: Yes
Handicapped Accessible: Yes
Food: In the vicinity
Bus Tours: Yes

Tukwila

Burlington Coat Factory
Pavilion Mall
24111 Highway 99

Directions: Call ahead.
Phone: (206) 575–3995
Hours: 9:30 A.M.–9:30 P.M., Monday–Friday; 9:30 A.M.–8:00 P.M., Saturday; 11:00 A.M.–6:00 P.M., Sunday
Additional Savings: Warehouse Coat Sale last two weeks of January
Credit Cards: American Express, Discover, MasterCard, Visa
Personal Checks: Yes
Handicapped Accessible: Yes
Food: Cucina Cucina, Azteca, and Winners restaurants all nearby
Bus Tours: Yes; arranged by mall management
Notes or Attractions: Close to Enchanted Village, Wild Waves, Seattle waterfront, Pike Place Market, and Seattle Center

Dress Barn
Pavilion Mall
17900 Southcenter Parkway

Directions: At Southcenter Parkway and South 180th, 1 mile south of the I–5/405 interchange
Phone: (206) 575–1916
Hours: 9:30 A.M.–9:30 P.M., Monday–Friday; 9:30 A.M.–8:00 P.M., Saturday; 11:00 A.M.–6:00 P.M., Sunday
Credit Cards: American Express, Discover, MasterCard, Optima, Visa
Personal Checks: Yes, with two forms of identification
Handicapped Accessible: Yes
Food: Food Pavilion on the second level
Bus Tours: Yes
Notes or Attractions: Two miles from Sea-Tac Airport; 5 miles from Seattle

JC Penney Furniture Warehouse Outlet
17200 Southcenter Parkway

Directions: From I–405, take Southcenter exit (S/C) and proceed to Southcenter Parkway; take a left and continue past Southcenter Mall about ⅓ mile; outlet is on the east side of the street. From I–5 southbound, take Southcenter exit and follow above directions. From I–5 northbound, take *first* Southcenter exit, take a right, and proceed on Southcenter Parkway.
Phone: (206) 575–4791
Hours: 9:30 A.M.–5:30 P.M., Monday–Saturday; 11:00 A.M.–5:00 P.M., Sunday
Additional Savings: Sale at the end of each month with further reductions on selected items
Credit Cards: American Express, JC Penney, MasterCard, Visa
Personal Checks: Yes
Handicapped Accessible: No
Food: Many fast-food and traditional restaurants along Southcenter Parkway
Bus Tours: No
Notes or Attractions: Southcenter Shopping Mall is just north. Green River Trail (bike and jogging path along Green River) is about 2 blocks east.

Nordstrom Rack
Pavilion Mall
17900 Southcenter Parkway

Directions: At Southcenter Parkway and South 180th, 1 mile south of the I–5/405 interchange
Phone: (206) 575–1058
Hours: 9:30 A.M.–9:30 P.M., Monday–Friday; 9:30 A.M.–8:00 P.M., Saturday; 11:00 A.M.–6:00 P.M., Sunday
Credit Cards: American Express, MasterCard, Visa
Personal Checks: Yes
Handicapped Accessible: Yes
Food: Food Pavilion on the second level
Bus Tours: Yes

Notes or Attractions: Two miles from Sea-Tac Airport; 5 miles from Seattle

Prestige Fragrance & Cosmetics
Pavilion Mall
17900 Southcenter Parkway

Directions: At Southcenter Parkway and South 180th, 1 mile south of the I-5/405 interchange
Phone: (206) 575-3991
Hours: 9:30 A.M.–9:30 P.M., Monday–Friday; 9:30 A.M.–8:00 P.M., Saturday; 11:00 A.M.–6:00 P.M., Sunday
Credit Cards: American Express, MasterCard, Visa
Personal Checks: Yes
Handicapped Accessible: Yes
Food: Food Pavilion on the second level
Bus Tours: Yes
Notes or Attractions: Two miles from Sea-Tac Airport; 5 miles from Seattle

Publishers Outlet
Pavilion Mall
17900 Southcenter Parkway

Directions: At Southcenter Parkway and South 180th, 1 mile south of the I-5/405 interchange
Phone: (206) 575-6424
Hours: 9:30 A.M.–9:30 P.M., Monday–Friday; 9:30 A.M.–8:00 P.M., Saturday; 11:00 A.M.–6:00 P.M., Sunday
Credit Cards: Discover, MasterCard, Visa
Personal Checks: Yes
Handicapped Accessible: Yes
Food: Food Pavilion on the second level
Bus Tours: Yes
Notes or Attractions: Two miles from Sea-Tac Airport; 5 miles from Seattle

Shoe Pavilion
Pavilion Mall
17900 Southcenter Parkway

Directions: At Southcenter Parkway and South 180th, 1 mile south of the I–5/405 interchange
Phone: (206) 575–0196
Hours: 9:30 A.M.–9:30 P.M., Monday–Friday; 9:30 A.M.–8:00 P.M., Saturday; 11:00 A.M.–6:00 P.M., Sunday
Credit Cards: American Express, Discover, MasterCard, Visa
Personal Checks: Yes (Washington only)
Handicapped Accessible: Yes
Food: Food Pavilion on the second level
Bus Tours: Yes
Notes or Attractions: Two miles from Sea-Tac Airport; 5 miles from Seattle

Studio Two
Pavilion Mall
17900 Southcenter Parkway

Directions: At Southcenter Parkway and South 180th, 1 mile south of the I–5/405 interchange
Phone: (206) 575–8852
Hours: 9:30 A.M.–9:30 P.M., Monday–Friday; 9:30 A.M.–8:00 P.M., Saturday; 11:00 A.M.–6:00 P.M., Sunday
Credit Cards: MasterCard, Visa
Personal Checks: Yes, with driver's license
Handicapped Accessible: Yes
Food: Food Pavilion on the second level
Bus Tours: Yes
Notes or Attractions: Two miles from Sea-Tac Airport; 5 miles from Seattle

Product Index

Clothing, Men's

**Clothing, Men's Career Wear/
    Formal Wear**

Clothing, Men's Casual Wear

Product Index

Outlet Index

Cabazon, 53
Folsom, 61
Gilroy, 65
Pacific Grove, 83
Vacaville, 133
WA: Burlington, 150

**Basic Brown Bear Factory
and Store**
CA San Francisco, 95–96

Basics Beauty Supply & Salon
CA: San Leandro, 121

Bass
CA: Anderson, 45
Barstow, 46
Cabazon, 53
Gilroy, 65
Lake Elsinore, 70
Mammoth Lakes, 77
Pacific Grove, 83
San Ysidro, 126
Truckee, 131
Vacaville, 133
OR: Lincoln City, 143
Troutdale, 146
WA: Centralia, 152
North Bend, 155

BC Jewelry and Gifts
CA: San Francisco, 115

Betty's Large Sizes
CA: Los Angeles, 73

Big Dogs Sportswear
CA: Barstow, 46

Bijoux Medici
CA: Commerce, 57

Bizmart
CA: San Leandro, 121

Black & Decker
CA: Barstow, 46
San Marcos, 122
San Ysidro, 126

Bon Worth
CA: San Marcos, 122
Vacaville, 133

Book Warehouse
CA: Anderson, 45
Barstow, 46
Commerce, 57
Folsom, 61
Mammoth Lakes, 77
Ontario, 82
Pacific Grove, 83
San Marcos, 122
San Ysidro, 126
Vacaville, 133
OR: Lincoln City, 143
Troutdale, 146
WA: North Bend, 155

Boot Factory/Genesco
CA: Barstow, 46
Vacaville, 133

Boston Traders
CA: Folsom, 61

Brands
CA: Gilroy, 65

Mall Index